T0311332

# MAGIC
## THE BASICS

*Magic: The Basics* is a concise and engaging introduction to magic in world history and contemporary societies. Presenting magic as a global phenomenon which has manifested in all human cultures, this book takes a thematic approach which explores the historical, social, and cultural aspects of magic.

Key features include:

- attempts to define magic either in universal or more particular terms, and to contrast it with other broad and potentially fluid categories such as religion and science;
- an examination of different forms of magical practice and the purposes for which magic has been used;
- debates about magic's effectiveness, its reality, and its morality;
- an exploration of magic's association with certain social factors, such as gender, ethnicity, and education, among others.

Offering a global perspective of magic from antiquity through to the modern era and including a glossary of key terms, suggestions for further reading, and case studies throughout, *Magic: The Basics* is essential reading for anyone seeking to learn more about the academic study of magic.

**Michael D. Bailey** is Professor of History at Iowa State University. He is founding co-editor of the journal *Magic, Ritual and Witchcraft* and has published extensively on the history of witchcraft and superstition in medieval Europe.

# THE BASICS

For a full list of titles in this series, please visit www.routledge.com/
The-Basics/book-series/B

# MAGIC

# THE BASICS

Michael D. Bailey

Routledge
Taylor & Francis Group

LONDON AND NEW YORK

First published 2018
by Routledge
2 Park Square, Milton Park, Abingdon, Oxon OX14 4RN

and by Routledge
711 Third Avenue, New York, NY 10017

*Routledge is an imprint of the Taylor & Francis Group, an informa business*

*British Library Cataloguing in Publication Data*
A catalogue record for this book is available from the British Library

*Library of Congress Cataloguing in Publication Data*
Names: Bailey, Michael David, 1971- author.
Title: Magic / Michael D. Bailey.
Description: 1 [edition]. | New York: Routledge, 2017. |
Series: The basics | Includes bibliographical references and index.
Identifiers: LCCN 2017010335 | ISBN 9781138809604
(hardback: alk. paper) | ISBN 9781138809611 (pbk.: alk. paper) |
ISBN 9781315749945 (ebook: alk. paper)
Subjects: LCSH: Magic.
Classification: LCC BF1611 .B26 2017 | DDC 133.4/3—dc23
LC record available at https://lccn.loc.gov/2017010335


ISBN: 978-1-138-80960-4 (hbk)
ISBN: 978-1-138-80961-1 (pbk)
ISBN: 978-1-315-74994-5 (ebk)


Typeset in Bembo
by codeMantra

For all my friends from London

# CONTENTS

# ACKNOWLEDGEMENTS

I am grateful to the College of Liberal Arts and Sciences at Iowa State University and its dean, Beate Schmittmann, whose Humanities Scholarship Enhancement Initiative afforded me time to finish this book amidst some pressing administrative duties. Thanks also to my colleagues and students in the History Department at Iowa State, who provided a receptive and responsive audience for some of my ideas. The readers for Routledge gave valuable feedback, and particularly at the proposal stage, they helped shape my thinking about this project. My thanks to them and the entire Routledge editorial team, who have been unfailingly helpful.

# INTRODUCTION: A MAGICAL WORLD

On midsummer nights in ancient Mesopotamia, ritual experts would perform a long and complex ceremony to undo harmful magic. Calling on the gods of night and on Night herself, "the veiled bride," they would burn images representing a wizard or witch in a brazier, turning those beings' wicked power back against them to protect their clients, who might be wealthy nobles or even kings.[1] When the Persian king Xerxes assailed Greece in the early fifth century BCE, the historian Herodotus relates, his great invasion fleet was stymied for three days by unrelenting storms. Finally, his priests quelled the tempest on its fourth day through incantations and sacrifices; "or perhaps," Herodotus casually remarks, "it abated on its own."[2] In fifteenth-century Europe, one magical text recommended that a sorcerer bite the heart out of a dove with his own teeth and use its blood to cast a love-spell.[3] Another, rather more respectably, laid out a rite invoking the Christian god to grant its practitioner knowledge "of any art whatsoever, and wisdom, memory, eloquence, intelligence, and understanding."[4] At the same time, some Europeans imagined that demonic witches were concocting poisons by mixing the juices of serpents, toads, or spiders with the boiled fat of murdered babies, that they could impede sexual intercourse, and that they could conjure hailstorms to destroy crops.[5]

Far beyond the boundaries of Europe, sorcerers in Han China (third century BCE to third century CE) also made use of both poisonous insects and evil spirits in their spells, while during the reign of the Qianlong Emperor in the eighteenth century something like a witch hunt broke out in response to fears that wandering sorcerers were stealing people's souls by magical means, and at the dawn of the twentieth century, participants in the Boxer Rebellion believed that spiritual entities would make them invulnerable to European weapons.[6] Among the Azande people of central Africa in the early twentieth century, healers would cure bewitchment by making an incision in their patients and apparently drawing out bewitched matter into a poultice. In modern South Africa, witches may attack someone by mixing graveyard earth with a magical potion and placing this concoction near the victim's house, while healers will craft their own potions and call on protective spirits to turn this harmful power back against the witch herself.[7] In other parts of Africa, conmen who make fantastic amounts of money via internet fraud or other means are often thought to be in league with occult forces, and people believe that witches now use invisible airplanes for their nighttime journeys.[8] In the modern Caribbean, migrant laborers have turned to spells to fortify themselves when traveling abroad for work, while other people have used magic to keep distant lovers faithful or to kill sexual rivals living in foreign lands.[9]

Magical beliefs and practices remain strong in modern Europe and North America as well. Occult societies of Rosicrucians, Theosophists, and others have flourished in both the Old World and the New. In the late nineteenth century, the famous Madame Blavatsky proclaimed the esoteric wisdom supposedly revealed to her by hidden Tibetan mahatmas, while in the early twentieth century the infamous Aleister Crowley, labeled "the wickedest man in the world" by the British press, combined sex and drugs with magical rites.[10] In Spain, *curanderos* dispensed love magic and healing charms, particularly against the evil eye, well into the twentieth century, and in 1926 a healer in the Netherlands was said to receive patients "almost daily."[11] In 1976, a court in England fined a man for sending a parcel containing a chicken's heart pierced with needles to his neighbor, who claimed it was a form of witchcraft meant to kill him.[12] In the early 2000s, a Gallup poll showed that more than twenty percent of people in the United States believed in witches, twenty-five percent believed in the power of astrology, more than forty percent believed in demonic possession, and more than fifty-percent believed in psychic or spiritual healing. All told, nearly three-quarters of Americans believed in at least some kind of "paranormal activity," compared to only half who believed in evolution.[13]

Of course, witches do exist in the modern world – self-proclaimed and proud. The neo-pagan religion of Witchcraft, also known as Wicca, developed in England in the mid-twentieth century but soon achieved great success throughout the Western world, especially in North America. Its followers stress its spiritual components but also assert their ability to work real magic. While Wicca and other forms of neo-paganism often emphasize their rootedness in the natural world, so-called techno-pagans embrace modern gadgets and gizmos into their rites, and neo-pagans of all kinds have found ways to adapt or develop rites for urban living, crafting spells to secure a parking place or to ensure a good WiFi connection, for example.

What are we to make of this array of examples that spans centuries and continents and still, of course, only scratches the surface of what has been or could be called magic across all human history? Intriguing connections abound, from seemingly parallel practices in very different contexts to similar reactions (often fear or derision, but also wonderment) expressed by widely separated societies and cultures. Some scholars contend that magic is so broad and diffuse a category that it becomes useless as a subject for any kind of analysis. What real similarity is there, after all, between a rite intended to heal an injury or illness and one intended to confer wisdom, secret knowledge or a glimpse into the future? What comparisons can be made between practices that explicitly call on supernatural spiritual entities and others that employ items from the natural world – herbs or stones, wooden wands or engraved metal images? And what connections really exist between complex rituals performed by experts in some craft, perhaps learned from arcane tomes written in obscure languages, and other acts that might be as simple as a muttered word, a gesture or even a baleful glance?

Obviously, this book takes the position that magic is a discernible aspect of human culture, and therefore a topic for serious analysis, however obscure and, by definition, occult it may be. The critics, however, have a point. Throughout much of history, magic has been a label and very often an accusation applied by certain people to the practices of others, whether that be members of one society deriding the rites and rituals of foreigners, or some powerful group within a society disparaging the behavior of the "common folk." The problems that color our perception of magic become even more complex when we consider other, potentially more sinister labels such as sorcery or witchcraft. It is mainly (although by no means exclusively) in the modern period that certain people have tried to reclaim these terms as emblems of positive and powerful identities. But they have been, and in some places still are, serious and potentially deadly accusations. Of course, this does not mean that people in the past did not claim great and mysterious powers, but they often referred to themselves by somewhat narrower titles: healer, diviner, exorcist, priest. Another valid complaint is that the term magic and many of its commonly employed cognates are Western in origin. We should be wary whenever we translate practices from other societies into Western terminology, and we must realize that Western structures of thought may not fully apply to them.

Nevertheless, magic seems to be here to stay, both as a category for academic study and, with endlessly variable connotations, as a term in common discourse as well. The point of this book will be to try to give some coherent form to those variations. We'll start, as we must, with words and definitions. No action is inherently magical. Instead, it comes to be understood as such only when some group of people declares it to be so and gets others to agree. While part of this book's focus will always be on the global scope of magic, when it comes to the words used to label this phenomenon the story will mainly be a Western one. This is inevitably so, in part, simply because this is a book written in English. More importantly, scholars from Europe and North America have done by far the most work to frame the academic study of magic in anthropology, history, religious studies, and other fields, and they have drawn mainly on the cache of words and concepts that Western history provides. Moreover, because of colonialism, imperialism, and lingering cultural hegemony, Western ideas and Western words now very deeply affect systems of thought, belief, and practice around the world. This, of course, further muddles our understanding of what magic can be, but as we'll see, that very uncertainty can become a place to start fixing our notions of the magical.

From words we'll switch to actions, framing the goals that the use of magic can be thought to achieve and the methods by which it is thought to be practiced. We'll also consider who typically is thought to employ magic, as well as the nature of the powers on which they are believed to draw. Then we'll move to reactions, examining how various societies have responded to what they have regarded as magical practices and practitioners. Again, while the overall focus will be global, a good deal of attention will be given to Western Europe, both because the European witch hunts from the fifteenth through the eighteenth centuries are probably the most spectacular (and certainly the most intensely studied) "reaction" to a set of perceived magical practices the world has ever known, and because the Christian condemnation of magic as diabolical continues to influence reactions around the world, as some evangelical pastors now inveigh against magic in Africa or Latin American as harshly as medieval preachers ever did.

In many societies, almost everyone will engage in some magical actions, at least on occasion, but they will not necessarily think of themselves as magicians for doing so. Also, however, across many cultures those who perform magic take it on, or have it ascribed to them, as a kind of identity. There can be many connotations, positive or negative, associated with that identity, and we'll explore the connections of magic to otherness, and to gender, in a few contexts. We'll also look at the vexed issue of whether magic is real. A staple of serious scholarship is that academics need not believe in magic themselves in order study it and to assert that belief in its reality has been a very important force throughout history and into the present day. We'll go beyond that, however, to explore how some kinds of magic might "really" (that is, empirically) work, and why so many people have believed in magic over time.

Finally, we'll explore magic in the modern world. This book isn't set up as a history and isn't meant to be read that way, but a key aspect of magic, certainly in the present day and to some extent throughout history as well, is how widely it has been thought of as "traditional" or even "primitive" and most definitely not modern. Thus, the concluding chapter on "Magic in the Modern World" frames not just a historical period but an important topic within the overall subject of magic.

I make no promise that, by the end of this book, everything you need to know about magic will have been made perfectly clear. One of the most basic elements of magic, we'll see again and again, is its inscrutability. We are dealing here, after all, with the occult, and it wouldn't do if at least a few shadows didn't remain even after much light has been cast. Throughout history and across cultures, magic most often exists at the point where the comfortably understood gives way to the mysteriously uncertain. That is what provides much of its allure and power. That is also what makes it such a fascinating subject to explore, and through which to explore a part of the human condition.

## NOTES

1  Tvzi Abusch, "Witchcraft Literature in Mesopotamia," in *The Babylonian World*, ed. Gwendolyn Leick (London: Routledge, 2007), 373–85.
2  Herodotus, *Histories* 7.191.
3  Richard Kieckhefer, *Forbidden Rites: A Necromancer's Manual from the Fifteenth Century* (University Park: Pennsylvania State University Press, 1998), 82.
4  Julien Véronèse, "Magic, Theurgy, and Spirituality in the Medieval Ritual of the *Ars notoria*," in *Invoking Angels: Theurgic Ideas and Practices, Thirteenth to Sixteenth Centuries*, ed. Claire Fanger (University Park: Pennsylvania State University Press, 2012), 57.
5  *Errores Gazariorum*, in Alan Charles Kors and Edward Peters, eds., *Witchcraft in Europe, 400–1700: A Documentary History*, 2nd ed. (Philadelphia: University of Pennsylvania Press, 2001), 161.
6  Xiaohuan Zhao, "Political Uses of Wugu Sorcery in Imperial China: A Cross-Cultural Perspective," *Magic, Ritual, and Witchcraft* 8 (2013): 133; Philip A. Kuhn, *Soulstealers: The Chinese Sorcery Scare of 1768* (Cambridge, MA: Harvard University Press, 1990).
7  Edward Evan Evans-Pritchard, *Witchcraft, Oracles, and Magic among the Azande*, abridged edition (Oxford: Oxford University Press, 1976), 102–104; Adam Ashforth, *Witchcraft, Violence, and Democracy in South Africa* (Chicago, IL: University of Chicago Press, 2005), 139–41.
8  Peter Geschiere, *Witchcraft, Intimacy, and Trust: Africa in Comparison* (Chicago, IL: University of Chicago Press, 2013), 56–57, 63–64.
9  Lara Putnam, "Rites of Power and Rumors of Race: The Circulation of Supernatural Knowledge in the Greater Caribbean, 1890–1940," in *Obeah and Other Powers: The Politics of Caribbean Religion and Healing*, ed. Diana Paton and Maarit Forde (Durham, NC: Duke University Press, 2012), 252–53.
10  Richard Kaczynski, *Perdurabo: The Life of Aleister Crowley*, rev. ed. (Berkeley, CA: North Atlantic Books, 2010), 394.

11 Enrique Perdiguero, "Magical Healing in Spain (1875–1936): Medical Pluralism and the Search for Hegemony," in *Witchcraft Continued: Popular Magic in Modern Europe*, eds. Willem de Blécourt and Owen Davies (Manchester: Manchester University Press, 2004), 133–50; Willem de Blécourt, "Boiling Chickens and Burning Cats: Witchcraft in the Western Netherlands, 1850–1925," in ibid., 98.

12 *Times* (London), June 19, 1976, p. 3.

13 www.gallup.com/poll/16915/three-four-americans-believe-paranormal. aspx#2 (accessed February 5, 2017); www.gallup.com/poll/170822/ believe-creationist-view-human-origins.aspx (accessed on February 5, 2017).

# 1

# THE MEANINGS OF MAGIC

Some kinds of magic can be called "black magic." Some can be called "white." But the issue of what magic "is" is rarely so simple. Magic can be black or white, but it can also be high or low, elite or common, learned or simple. It can be ritual, ceremonial, sympathetic, or contagious. Magic can be performed by magicians, of course, but also by sorcerers, witches, wizards, warlocks, enchanters, shamans, conjurors, and illusionists. To be a victim of witchcraft sounds terrible, but to be bewitched by something sounds a bit better, and to be enchanted sounds quite nice indeed. The French philosopher Voltaire, writing in the eighteenth century, quipped that while the Christian church had always condemned magic, "she always believed in it" as well, and he noted more basically that the religious beliefs and practices of one sect were considered superstitious and magical by others.[1] At the opposite end of one possible spectrum, the twentieth-century science fiction author Arthur C. Clarke's famous Third Law holds that "any sufficiently advanced technology is indistinguishable from magic."[2]

Few things that loom so large in human culture are as hard to pin down precisely as the concept of magic. Most people know what magic means, or at least what it implies, in most general contexts, but scratch the surface of any discussion, and problems start to bubble up. In scholarly circles, certainly, no broad definition of magic as a category of academic study has ever been without controversy. This is not (just) due to the penchant scholars have for picking apart each other's arguments. Rather, it stems from the fact that magic, throughout its long history in most human cultures, has been a deeply contested category and a very fraught label. While some people have explicitly claimed that they possessed magical powers, many others have stood accused of practicing magic, often by authorities intent on punishing them in some fairly severe ways. Naturally, they have tried to defend themselves against this charge, and they have frequently done so not by denying any particular actions but by claiming that those actions are not magic, as authorities understand it, or that they represent good magic rather than bad.

These dynamics mean that any thorough exploration of this topic needs to include some discussion of the various meanings that magic can convey and the many names that can be given to magical practices. Here, we'll look first at the relationship of magic to other broad framing categories, namely religion and science, followed by an exploration of how scholars have tried to create general definitions of magic that can serve to differentiate it from these other categories. Then we'll turn to the word "magic" itself and the multitude of other terms that have been used to label magical practices, limited first just to the context of Western, mainly European, civilization, and then addressing some of the further problems that arise when Western terminology is applied more broadly around the globe. Finally, I'll suggest a solution to these dilemmas, which is to embrace this tangle of meanings as something that is essential to the definition of magic in all contexts.

## MAGIC, RELIGION, AND SCIENCE

People around the world have struggled with the meanings of magic, and continue to do so, because understanding magic can be extremely important. In the broadest sense, it can provide a framework for thinking about both the physical world and the spiritual universe. Scholars sometimes use phrases like "magical thinking" or a "magical worldview." As such, magic has often been set in contrast with other, equally capacious frameworks (and, one might add, equally fluid too), at least in Western thought.

Troublesome as fixed definitions of magic are, we must begin somewhere. Let's start with the proposition that magic should be understood as a set of practices intended to influence or control either mystical, spiritual forces or physical properties that exist within nature but are hidden or occult, that is, not readily apparent or available to all people. This definition covers a lot of ground and might serve nicely in many ways, but immediately a problem is also apparent. Not all practices designed to do these things, either through the course of human history or in the present day, have been thought of as magical. Rituals to control, placate, or supplicate spiritual powers can be thought of as religious in many contexts, while the manipulation of often invisible natural forces can bring us into the realm of science. The opposition of magic to both religion, on the one hand, and science, on the other, has been critically important to how all three categories have been understood over the course of Western history.

As Voltaire noted, it has been common throughout history for one group of people to regard the religious practices of other groups as magic. In fact, the root of the word "magic" in Western languages originated with the ancient Greeks and was used to describe the practices of the Persian priestly class, the *magoi*. People in ancient polytheistic cultures believed that the world was inhabited by multitudes of powerful spirits. Foreign gods were typically thought to be strange and perhaps more disreputable than one's own, but they were real and powerful nonetheless. Likewise, the priests of other cultures could be considered somewhat nefarious, but their practices could still be regarded as effective. The Greeks had their own gods of magic, including Artemis, known as Diana to the Romans, but most especially Hecate, a goddess of the moon, magic, and witchcraft. She was (or became) a horrifying figure. The third-century BCE poet Theocritus describes her, in his *Idylls*, creeping through burial sites while frightened dogs quake at her approach, and she is also depicted killing women in childbirth.[3] Among her priestesses was the foreign princess Medea, a sorceress who performed monstrous deeds during her unhappy marriage to the Greek hero Jason, including in some versions of the myth killing her own children.

The ancient Hebrews also often ascribed what could be called magic to the priests of foreign cultures. In the biblical Book of Exodus, for example, Moses and Aaron challenged Pharaoh to release the Hebrews from bondage in Egypt. They performed a number of wondrous signs (or the Hebrew god performed wonders through them), such as transforming rods into serpents or causing the Nile to flow red with blood. These were initially matched by the "wise men and sorcerers...the magicians of Egypt" through their "secret arts."[4] On the eve of a major battle against the Philistines, the Hebrew king Saul consulted a diviner, later known as "the witch" of Endor, only after he had tried to consult his own priests but "the Lord did not answer him."[5] Similar parallels are found in other cultures. Practices subsequently considered to be magic in ancient India were often associated with gods, mystics, or holy men. In ancient China, the kinds of rites that would be labeled magic in the West were thought of as various kinds of "arts" (*shu*), some of which were the special purview of shamans or monks. As late as the eighteenth century, a major "sorcery" scare in China (although Chinese lacks that specific word) focused in part on Buddhist monks and Taoist priests.[6] In Mesoamerican societies prior to Spanish conquest, gods and spirits were typically seen as ambivalent figures, not entirely good or evil. After the conquest, native people themselves readily identified some of these figures with Christian demons or the devil, and hence with Christian ideas of magic, but still worshiped or at least invoked them through traditional rites.[7]

Monotheistic cultures tend to draw more fundamental distinctions between magic and religion, and none has done so with more enduring consequences than Christianity. In the strict dichotomy of the Christian universe, God worked miracles and edifying wonders. All other marvelous actions were magic, which Christian authorities resolutely linked to the devil. As the seventh-century bishop Isidore of Seville would write, all the "magic arts" had "issued from a certain pestilential alliance of humans and evil angels."[8] When it came to categorizing different actions – such as a healing rite, a spoken blessing, or a muttered curse – as either magical or religious, this distinction was not always so easily drawn by Christian authorities, nor so readily understood by many Christians. But in theory, the separation was absolute. Eventually, Europeans would export their ideas of magic not just as something foreign or vaguely mysterious but as profoundly evil and corrupt around the world. The process is still ongoing today, as some Pentecostal missionaries in Africa or Latin America proclaim that anyone practicing traditional forms of medicine, divination, or other arts is in fact ensnared in diabolical witchcraft. In some cases, though, people have fought back, reasserting (or claiming for the first time) religious validation for various practices. For example, Vodou, which began as condemned *voodoo* and *sortilège* in Haiti, now has the status of an official religion. And in both Europe and North America since the mid-twentieth century, self-proclaimed Witches or Wiccans have crafted a religious system that incorporates practices that they explicitly deem to be magical.

If boundaries between magic and religion have proven to be fluid and uncertain over time and across cultures, are distinctions between magic and science any more stable? Modern Western science has sought to distance itself from magic just as much if not more than modern Western religions have. The vehemence of committed partisans can be just as extreme. Physicist Robert Park declares, for example, that "science is the only way of knowing – everything else is just superstition."[9] Into this category, one must presume that Park would group anything he considered to be magical (and probably a good deal of religion as well). Such attitudes have a long pedigree. In antiquity, too, educated elites often derided magical practices in light of what they regarded as sound scientific knowledge. Perhaps no early "scientist" is more famous, in this regard, than the Roman writer and natural philosopher Pliny the Elder, who died while observing the eruption of Mount Vesuvius in 79 CE. In his great compendium the *Natural History*, he castigated many practices that could be considered magical, including the explicit "magic" of Persian *magoi*, whom he considered charlatans. In particular, he condemned what he regarded as false healing practices, contrasting this "magic" to the true power of legitimate medicine.

Pliny, however, was not really distinguishing between two entirely separate approaches to healing; rather he was just labeling those practices he thought were effective and appropriate as "medicine" and those he thought were inefficacious and foolish as "magical" or "superstitious." Later physicians and scientists would come to consider many beliefs and practices of which he approved to be misinformed and magical. For example, he maintained that anyone stung by a scorpion would never thereafter be stung by any other animal, such as a hornet, wasp, or bee, and he also felt that spitting on epileptics could help cure their seizures. Against snakebites, the spittle of a person who was fasting was especially efficacious.[10] Similarly, Pliny contrasted many false and "magical" forms of divination with what he thought were appropriate methods of prognostication, but few of these would survive scientific scrutiny today. Throughout subsequent centuries, educated elites continued to deride various forms of magic as foolish superstition, even as they were deeply fearful of other kinds of magic, and even as they may have practiced some kinds of magic themselves.

Even in the era of Europe's Scientific Revolution, in the later sixteenth and seventeenth centuries, proponents of new scientific methods might castigate certain kinds of magical practices that they thought were grounded in erroneous knowledge or a false understanding of the natural world, but they did not proclaim any absolute separation between magical and scientific thought. In fact, just as in Pliny's day, they often still supported what would later come to be regarded as profoundly magical beliefs. One example of this is Joseph Glanvill, an English clergyman but also a natural philosopher and early member of the Royal Society. In his work *Saducismus Triumphatus* (Sadducism Conquered), published in its final form in 1681, he defended the existence of spiritual forces in the physical world from a scientific viewpoint, drawing in part on witch trials as his empirical evidence. Another member of the Royal Society, Robert Boyle (1627–1691), considered to be one of the fathers of modern chemistry and famous for Boyle's Law of gas pressure, could just as easily be labeled an alchemist. He corresponded with many other famous adherents of alchemy in this era, including the political philosopher John Locke and mathematician and physicist Isaac Newton. Now often regarded as the culminating figure of the Scientific Revolution, Newton's reputation was not quite so set in his own day. His famous theory of gravity, for example, was derided as an "occult" notion by the rival German mathematician Gottfried Wilhelm Leibniz because it posited an invisible force that operated by unseen mechanisms over great distances.

Beyond these individual examples of major scientific figures blurring any clear or absolute boundaries between magic and science, it is useful also to consider one of the major shifts that occurred in the realm of "science" during Europe's early modern era. Much of the revolutionary work of the Scientific Revolution was achieved through startling new empirical observations and measurements. This was no longer the straightforward Aristotelian observation and categorization of the visible world that had characterized ancient and medieval natural philosophy, however. Now carefully designed experiments were needed to expose the "secrets" of nature, that is, aspects of the natural world that were not immediately observable except under very specific conditions. This development was accompanied by a shift in how European intellectuals regarded natural curiosities and wonders – anything from unusual mutations in plants to monstrous births in animals to comets blazing across the otherwise well-ordered heavens. Whereas before these had been taken as demonstrations of supernatural intervention in nature, they now came to be regarded as evidence of the entirely natural but heretofore hidden workings of the world. As "occult" properties in nature, such phenomena had long been associated with the realm of magic. In a sense, early modern science, rather than distancing itself from magic, had invaded and taken over part of magic's former domain.

None of this should be taken to dismiss the obvious distance that now separates modern science from most conceptions of magic, but it does demonstrate that this sharp separation is quite a recent development and that such distinctions were more complex through most of human history. We tend to misread history, in fact, by projecting the label of "science" back onto only that portion of premodern natural philosophy, medical art, or other forms of learning that conform to our current notions of what science is. This habit developed in Europe, but a particularly dramatic illustration of the process may be seen in colonial India. At the end of the nineteenth century, native elites in the subcontinent, impressed by the progress that British science and technology had produced, sought to demonstrate that Indian thinking was every bit as scientific as that which came from the West. To this end, they engaged in a project to purify Hinduism of what they considered to be superstitious accretions: a multiplicity of gods, temples, and cultic practices, as well as mysticism and magic. If all this could be successfully stripped away, they argued, the core of Hinduism found in the ancient Vedic texts would be seen to be as rational and amenable to modern science as the European philosophical tradition grounded in classical antiquity (a notion that was itself based on nineteenth-century dogma that the ancient Greeks and Romans had been rational and scientific in a modern sense).[11] In their idealistic and well-intentioned efforts, we can see just how hazy the boundaries between magic, religion, and science have often been, and how our sense of sharp difference is often the result of entirely after-the-fact impositions.

## UNIVERSALIZING ATTEMPTS IN ANTHROPOLOGY AND SOCIOLOGY

European scholars began to confront the problems and imprecisions in their categories of magic, religion, and science in the late nineteenth and early twentieth centuries. As anthropologists and then sociologists began to explore magic around the globe, they realized that the grounds for distinguishing magic from religion bequeathed to them by centuries of Christian culture did not easily or accurately apply. Convinced that absolute categorizations were still possible, however, they sought to develop them with academic rigor. None of these systems long withstood the test of time, but these men remain great names in the early history of the modern study of magic, and their theories are often still used as starting points for academic inquiry, even if only as straw men to be quickly demolished. For this reason, they deserve some of our attention here.

Edward Tylor (1832–1917) was the first professor of anthropology at Oxford University and is often considered "the father of Anthropology" as an academic field.[12] He presented his influential ideas about magic mainly in his major work *Primitive Cultures* (1871), and his theories were evolutionary. He considered magic to be rooted in animism (the notion that all things are animated by spirit powers), which he considered to be an early stage of human belief, out of which humanity, or segments thereof (mainly Western Europeans), evolved over time toward more advanced forms of religion, culminating in monotheism. All remnants of magic were merely survivals of this original primitive culture, and he considered them "pernicious delusions" and a "monstrous farrago."[13] Although the label of "the primitive" no longer sits well with anthropologists or historians, his notion that belief in magic represents an early stage of human development out of which the species (or in later psychological theories, the individual) should naturally grow has had enduring power. It does not, however, fit the actual course of historical development in most human societies.

Another Englishman, James Frazer, influenced not just academic debate but popular culture as well with his sprawling, multi-volume and multi-edition masterpiece *The Golden Bough* (three editions 1890–1915, although probably best known through Frazer's own one-volume abridgment in 1922). Here, he propounded an even more developed evolutionary model than Tylor had, advancing humanity in stages from magic to religion to science, but he also allowed for significant overlaps between these stages. In explaining how magical rites were thought to operate, Frazer posited two basic mechanisms. In the case of magical sympathy, ritual actions are believed to cause symbolically similar events. For example, a witch might stir a pool of water to cause a storm at sea. In the case of magical contagion, items brought together or linked in some ritual way are believed to continue to affect each other even after they are separated. Building on Tylor's ideas about animism, Frazer recognized that magic often aimed to interact with spiritual powers, but he argued that magical systems functioned or at least were set up to function as if those powers would always respond in set ways to set practices.

In this, ironically, magic struck Frazer as being somewhat akin to science, in that it regarded the universe as ordered into fixed structures that always reacted in the same way if manipulated correctly. Magic differed from science, however, in that it was based on fundamentally incorrect understandings of natural processes. Thus, it represented only a primitive and false attempt at what science would later achieve. Religion for Frazer, on the other hand, reflected a very different notion that powerful spiritual entities shape the universe and act within it in ways beyond human understanding. For him, religious belief represented an advance over magical thinking because it demonstrated that humans had come to recognize the falsity and futility of magical rites. This was reflected by the fact that while magicians sought to control powerful spiritual forces, priests worshiped and propitiated higher powers without expecting any automatic response. Frazer admitted, however, that magical practices could and typically did endure in societies long after they had also developed what he regarded as religious systems.

In 1902, the French sociologist Marcel Mauss (1872–1950) published a long essay on "A General Theory of Magic" with fellow sociologist Henri Hubert. Here, he moved away from quasi-biological notions of evolution and differentiated magic from religion based on the social role it played. While religious ceremonies are open and public in this scheme, magic is performed secretively and in isolation. As Mauss wrote, "magical rites are commonly performed in woods, far away from dwelling places, at night, or in shadowy corners."[14] Thus magic is conceived to be an essentially private craft. While it might be performed by groups in certain circumstances, it cannot develop real institutional structures like temples or priesthoods. For this reason, it can never obtain official sanction or broad-based support in any society, and in fact, it is often condemned by religious or other authorities as a threat to social order. With these social distinctions in place, however, Mauss could envision significant overlap between magical practices and religious ones, and he had no difficulty explaining how both magic and religion could develop side by side in the same society.

This manner of differentiating magic from religion was amplified by Mauss's famous uncle, Émile Durkheim (1858–1917), who defined his idea of religion in part through an opposition to magic in his major study of *The Elementary Forms of Religious Life* (1912). He too recognized that magic and religion often operate through similar forms or structures, such as "ceremonies, sacrifices, purifications, prayers, songs and dances."[15] They also often claim to draw on similar or identical sources of power. But they are frequently locked in opposition to one another, with religious authorities condemning magic and magicians either deliberately or indirectly subverting religious principles through their rites. Religion, for Durkheim, binds groups together and unifies them into communities of belief and practice (churches), but magic is, if not always directly antisocial, more practical and utilitarian in its ends. Again, magical practices may be performed by groups, and magical beliefs may be widespread among a given population, but these do not create any sense of community. "In history we do not find religion without Church," writes Durkheim, but "there is no Church of magic."[16]

The last great theorist of magic in the early twentieth century was the Polish-born anthropologist Bronislaw Malinowski (1884–1942). He did important field work in the Trobriand Islands in Melanesia during World War I, and drawing on this he published his most influential essay on "Magic, Science, and Religion" in 1925. Unlike Mauss, he saw valuable social functions in magic. It can offer solutions in situations where ordinary human capacities or knowledge are inadequate. In a sense, religion does this too, but at a very different level. Moving beyond Durkheim's notion of religion as a social force creating community, Malinowski defined religion as transcendent. It addresses the greatest issues humanity confronts: life and death, morality, and so forth. Its rites and rituals are not intended to achieve direct, mundane ends but rather come to take on a higher value in and of themselves. Magical rites, by contrast, remain far more limited and practical. They seek to achieve specific goals and alleviate specific problems, and they must accomplish this, or at least appear to do so, in order to have value. They impart no transcendent meaning and so have no worth in and of themselves. In this sense, Malinowski, like Frazer, sees magic as a technique somewhat related to science, although also like Frazer he regards it to be incorrect in its underlying premises of cause and effect, and so it is only a "pseudo-science."[17]

Malinowski's student E. E. Evans-Pritchard (1902–1973) was not a theorist of magic or religion. He was very much a field anthropologist who did his doctoral research among the Azande people of the upper Nile in Africa. His major work emerging from this was *Witchcraft, Oracles, and Magic among the Azande* (1937). Although it initially had little impact on scholarship, in the decades after World War II, it became extremely influential among both anthropologists and historians.[18] Proceeding from native categories, Evans-Pritchard identified as "witchcraft" what the Azande called *mangu*, which was a physical substance within certain people, passed on through heredity, that gave them malevolent powers. In contrast, more general "magic" was *ngua*, a means of employing mystical power through rites and via natural materials, and which, in sharp contrast to *mangu*, was a skill that its practitioners had to learn. For Evans-Pritchard, *ngua* used to harm was "sorcery." Finally, *soroka* were "oracles," means to divine the future or learn otherwise undiscoverable information. He stressed that even harmful witchcraft or sorcery could serve a socially useful function by providing an explanation for otherwise inexplicable misfortunes, and a possible means of redress if the culprit could be found. While he had no intention of expanding his categories into a universally applicable system, many other scholars have found his distinctions useful.

Evans-Pritchard proved to be something of a bellwether in that, in the second half of the twentieth century, scholars in various disciplines turned increasingly to the topic of harmful witchcraft rather than magic in general. They also shied away from advancing general theories about what magic is or was in favor of focused studies of magical practices in specific contexts. For a time, a strong comparative emphasis remained even among this sort of scholarship. Notably anthropological studies of African witchcraft, and especially the work of Evans-Pritchard himself, reignited historical study of European witchcraft and the early modern witch hunts of the sixteenth and seventeenth centuries, now approached from the perspective of social history rather than religious or church history, which had previously been the norm. Eventually, however, specificity won out, with historians emphasizing the unique conditions that had shaped European witchcraft, above all those imposed by Christianity and its powerful demonization of magic, while anthropologists and other scholars focused on Africa or Asia grew leery of using European categories to frame their own studies.[19] To understand these specificities and the problems that they in turn engendered, we need now to enter into the terminology of magic and witchcraft as it evolved in Europe, and then to the various ways that this language has been and continues to be imposed onto beliefs and practices around the globe.

## WESTERN TERMINOLOGY OVER TIME

As we've already seen, the word "magic" comes from the ancient Greeks. They described the rites of the Persian *magoi* as *magikos*, which became *magicus* for the Romans. These terms did not remain restricted to the practices of Eastern priests for very long, however. At roughly the same time that the historian Herodotus was recounting how *magoi* might perhaps conjure up or disperse storms at sea (fifth century BCE), the playwright Sophocles put the word *magos* into the mouth of his tragic hero Oedipus, who hurled it as an insult at the native Greek prophet Tiresias, when the seer's predictions had angered the king.[20] In fact, Tiresias was a *mantis*, a diviner in Greek terminology, although Oedipus, when angry, also calls him an *agurtes*, a wandering beggar-priest. Clearly, Sophocles was playing with the somewhat slippery boundaries that existed between these words, and he clearly shows that *mageia* was no longer an epithet reserved solely for Persian practices.

Neither, however, was *mageia* the catch-all category that modern "magic" can imply. The Greeks had many other words, all possessing both specific meanings and vaguer implications. Standing alongside the *magos* and the *mantis*, one could add the *goes*, a practitioner of *goeteia*. Originally having to do with burial rites and ritual laments, divination, and healing, this term expanded to include dark magical practices of any kind. It is very often translated into English as "witchcraft." Similarly, the practice of *pharmakeia* meant the use of *pharmakon*, which was a drug or medicinal substance of any kind. Although these substances could be used to heal as well as harm, *pharmakeia* often carried an implication of poisoning, which then blended into connotations of harmful magic and witchcraft. While they retained their distinct meanings, these words also all became interrelated over time, in ways that scholars are still trying to understand from fragmentary sources spanning many centuries. Because of these complexities, scholars of Western antiquity often bristle as much as do anthropologists focusing on the non-Western world about using the modern terminology of "magic" or "witchcraft" to describe ancient practices, but outside of highly technical scholarship, there seems no escaping it.[21]

The Romans had their own terminology and their own conceptual schemes, frequently paralleling those of the Greeks. *Carmen*, for example, was a song but also a spell or incantation (which would have been *epaoide* in Greek). *Veneficium* referred to poisoning or use of drugs, potions, or other substances to harm, and like the Greek *pharmakeia* it is often translated as "witchcraft." Having borrowed their terms *magus/magicus/magia* from the Greeks, the Romans continued to apply these words to Persian practices for a long time. That remains the sense in which the orator Cicero (106–43 BCE) used them in the mid-first century BCE. Not much later, however, the poet Virgil (70–19 BCE) used the adjective *magicus* to refer to powerful rites intended to compel love in his eighth *Eclogue*. By the mid-first century CE, "magic" seems to have become a general category for the Romans. Pliny the Elder designated an array of what he considered to be false or erroneous beliefs and practices as *magicae vanitates* (magical vanities). Most often he contrasted this vain magic to proper medicine, but he also used the term to encompass divinatory practices and other ritual techniques. By the late imperial period, Roman law codes labeled criminal forms of magic used to cause harm as *maleficia* (meaning "evil deeds"). This would become the principal term for witchcraft used throughout

Western Europe by Latin-educated authorities in the medieval and early modern periods.

With the rise of Christianity and the transition from the ancient to the medieval period of Western history, the terminology and conceptualizations of magic became somewhat simpler. "Magic" was now a relatively broad and encompassing category, designated either by the word *magia* itself or more often as *artes magicae*, the magic arts. Conceptually, as we have seen, Christian authorities maintained that all magical practices, however different they might appear, were inherently related to each other in that all or at least the great majority of them drew in some way on the malevolent power of demons. In fact, however, medieval authorities writing about magic could and did still deploy a dizzying array of varied but interrelated terms. One of the greatest of medieval list-makers, the early-seventh-century bishop Isidore of Seville, whom we have already met, provided an extensive catalog of kinds of magic in the section of his *Etymologies* titled "On Magicians" (*De magis*). Here, he discussed augury, oracles, necromancy, astrology, horoscopes, amulets, and incantations among many other forms of practice. He also discussed people known as *sortilegi*, who cast lots (*sortes*). This word would expand its meaning over time to encompass all sorts of divinatory practices and then other kinds of magical practices as well. From the later Latin, *sorceria* would come the French *sorcellerie* and ultimately the English word "sorcery."

Of all medieval terms for magic, *maleficium* undoubtedly underwent the most important shift in connotation, if not in underlying meaning. Medieval Christian writers took this word from Roman legal authorities as their most basic term for magic used to harm or otherwise commit wicked acts. It is usually rendered into English as "sorcery" or even more often as "witchcraft." *Malefici*, those who performed *maleficium*, could come from any level of medieval society, but generally they were ordinary, uneducated people, and very often they were women. Later in the medieval era, primarily in the fifteenth century, a *malefica* became more than just a woman who performed harmful magic, inevitably demonic in the Christian conception of things, in isolation from others. Instead, legal and religious authorities began to imagine that numerous *maleficae* now operated as members of diabolical sects, periodically gathering together to worship demons, receive instructions from them, and perform various other abominations such as murdering and cannibalizing young children and desecrating Christian sacraments. This notion of conspiratorial witchcraft was encapsulated in several texts, including the infamous witch-hunting manual *Malleus Maleficarum* (The Hammer of Witches), written in 1486. Although this stereotype was never static and never universally accepted across Europe, it still underlays most of the major witch hunts that Europe experienced through the sixteenth and seventeenth centuries. The satanic conspiracy imagined lying behind this crime was very important in driving many of those hunts, because under this conception of witchcraft, any convicted witch could be expected to name others of her sect, and, in most jurisdictions, could be forced to do so through the application of torture.

The later Middle Ages was also the period when various words for "witch" developed in most of the vernacular languages of Europe, including *sorcière* in French and *Hexe* in German. Initially, a witch could also be a *vaudois* in French or *Unholde* in German, but these terms did not attain the necessary traction to survive as common appellations down through the centuries. What became the typical Italian word for a witch, *strega*, derived from the Latin *striga*, also meaning a witch, but which itself derived from *strix*, the name for the screech owl but also designating a vampiric monster that roamed the night and murdered children by draining them of their blood. Italian notions of witchcraft (*stregoneria*) retained certain elements of vampirism throughout the medieval and early modern periods. Similar connotations clung to the Spanish *bruja* and her performance of *brujería*, but they are not nearly so common in the Northern European terminology for witchcraft. In English, "witch" derives from the Old English *wicce*. Originally, this may have meant a soothsayer or diviner, but it also carried dangerous connotations of harmful magic, and these were certainly amplified over time.

We needn't chase these words too far into the modern period, as their meanings become more clearly those that are most familiar to us now. Even in the modern period, however, and outside of academic word-wars, some contestation and dispute about the meanings of various words have continued. The early-twentieth-century British occultist Aleister Crowley, for example, insisted on the spelling "magick" to differentiate what he defined as "the science and art of causing change to occur in conformity with will" from the illusions and tricks of stage performers.[22] The very need to designate certain magic as "stage magic" indicates the range of not always compatible meanings that the word can still convey. Even more serious debates have swirled around witchcraft. As the neo-pagan religion of modern Witchcraft (usually capitalized) has developed in the later twentieth and early twenty-first centuries, practitioners have had to decide whether they want to be called Witches or Wiccans. Some have preferred the latter term, specifically to avoid the negative connotations that being called a witch conveys. Others demand to be called a Witch, deliberately seeking to reappropriate the word. Still others distinguish between Wiccans, who have been initiated into particular traditions of their faith, and Witches, who may be independent or solitary practitioners.[23]

## WESTERN TERMINOLOGY IN GLOBAL CONTEXTS

While the terminology that has been applied to magical practices is complicated enough even when limited to Western history, problems only magnify when European categories are applied to other cultures. European powers began to colonize other regions of the world in major ways in the sixteenth century, and they exported their conceptions of magic and especially witchcraft as they did so. Particularly in sub-Saharan Africa and the Americas, Europeans regarded natives as primitive savages. They made little effort (although they did make some) to understand indigenous beliefs and practices. A possibility existed that, even while regarding natives as primitive, European conquerors might see them as noble savages living, albeit unaware, in divinely ordained natural innocence. This is not, however, what usually happened. Instead, colonizing authorities came to see native practices as diabolical magic or witchcraft that Christian religion needed to stamp out. This process typically meant recasting inherently ambivalent native beliefs and practices as completely evil, along with a corresponding shift in words and meanings. For example, in Andean regions formerly controlled by the Incan Empire, the word *supay* referred to morally neutral spirits that could cause either harm or good. Under Spanish domination, however, it came to mean an entirely evil demon or the Christian devil, a meaning that it retains in the modern

Quechua language in Peru, where a common curse is to call someone a *supaypa wawan*, or "child of the devil." Likewise, a perhaps somewhat malevolent spirit known as *hapinuñu* transformed under the influence of the new colonial rulers into a female nighttime monster that preyed on children, very much like a European witch, especially in the Mediterranean mold of the *bruja* or *strega*.[24]

European terminology could itself undergo interesting transformations as it came to be deployed around the world, intermingling with indigenous categories or influencing completely new concepts. The notion of a West African "fetish" object, for instance, comes from the Portuguese words *feitiçaria*, often translated as sorcery, and *feitiço*, meaning a spell. Portuguese explorers were the first Europeans to sail down the African coast and introduce these terms to that region. Subsequently, however, Europeans who came into contact with West African tribes understood a *fetiche* as an African term and concept. In the eighteenth century, in fact, even a Portuguese dictionary posited that the word *feitiço* might have derived from the African *fetiche* rather than recognizing that the influence went the other way around.[25]

Tendencies like these have continued into more recent times, when the forces of European colonialism and imperialism grew even more powerful across much of the world, even if they sometimes manifested in less direct ways. Here we can return to the case of the British anthropologist E. E. Evans-Pritchard and his fieldwork among the Azande in Africa in the early twentieth century. He was a careful scholar who clearly sought to understand rather than reshape native categories. Nevertheless, he still decided to apply European labels to African practices. What the Azande called *mangu*, in which malevolent power derived from a material substance physically present within certain people, he labeled "witchcraft." He understood *ngua*, in which power is derived from the application of medicinal substances often accompanied by some rite, such as a spell or incantation, as magic more generally. When *ngua* was used to harm, which the Azande certainly understood as a concept, he called this practice "sorcery." But in fact, the Azande did not have a wholly distinct word for that negative magical action, instead calling it *gbegere ngua* or *kitikiti ngua* (bad magic).

Neither do the forces of colonialism always need to work only through the colonizers. The colonized themselves frequently play a role in transforming their own thought and language to better match what some come to accept as more advanced categories derived from the modern West. I have mentioned already how, in the nineteenth century, Indian elites sought to purge Hinduism of what they regarded as magical or superstitious elements, so that it would more closely conform to European ideas of religion. Even earlier, and half a world away, almost immediately after the successful Haitian revolution in 1804, Jean-Jacques Dessalines, independent Haiti's first ruler, began to suppress the ritual gatherings known as *danses de vodou* by military force. By 1835, Hatian legal codes categorized all Vodou as *sortilège* (sorcery/witchcraft), even though within the Vodou tradition a separate category of *maji* existed to describe specifically malevolent or harmful practices. The government intended that this official, self-imposed condemnation of native practices would help to position Haiti among the "civilized" nations of the world.

Of course, as we marvel at the nature of these enforced transformations of meanings, as well as the unplanned changes that occurred more naturally over time, we should not think that any native terminology will necessarily be any more precise than imposed European categories. The Pondo people of South Africa, for example, have a distinction similar to that which Evans-Pritchard identified among the Azande, namely that harmful magic can either derive from some inherent force within a person (witchcraft) or that it can stem from a magical/medicinal practice using potions, spells, and other components of a learned craft (sorcery). But the Pondo don't have separate words for these categories. Their term *ukuthakatha* applies to either kind of practice, and the words *umthakathi* and *igqwira* can both mean either sorcerer or witch, in this sense.[26]

The Pondo are Xhosa-speaking. Zulu and Sotho speakers in South Africa often refer to assaults by witches as *idliso* and *sejeso.* Both words derive from the root verb "to eat" in their respective languages, and in the most literal sense both refer to poisoning. In other words, we see here a sort of "witchcraft" that might just as well be categorized as "sorcery" in other schemes. This is precisely the sort of distinction that academics might feel is very important to draw. Focusing only on Zulu, scholars studying magical practices often distinguish *inyanga* from *sangoma*. These terms mean, respectively, a man (usually) who uses traditional medicines and practices to perform his craft (so, a "herbalist") and a woman (usually) who has clairvoyant powers and communicates with spirits and ancestors (so, a "diviner"). The concepts would appear to be quite different, but in common usage, among Zulu speakers, these terms are most often completely interchangeable.[27]

Among the Maka of southern Cameroon, native speakers regularly translate their word *djambe* into French as *sorcellerie*, or witchcraft, and they frequently use the word *sorcellerie* itself even when speaking in their native tongue rather than French. But in fact, as we have seen with witchcraft elsewhere in Africa, here *djambe* is envisioned as a creature living inside certain people that gives them their special powers. A *djindjamb* is someone who has cultivated this capability and can be described as a witch. To complicate matters further, traditional healers among the Maka, known as *nganga*, are also thought to possess *djambe*, and they claim this themselves.[28] Although they position themselves against the malevolent powers of witches, they also frequently call themselves *sorciers*, which could be translated as "sorcerers," but, since this is just the male form of *sorcière* in French, meant to refer to a practitioner of *sorcellerie*, they might just as well be called witches. In fact, the Maka are playing on uncertainty and tension that manifest in similar although maybe not precisely identical ways in both their own language and that of their European colonizers.

## EMBRACING UNCERTAINTY

In some circumstances, people who engage in magical practices can quite deliberately play word-games, exploiting the uncertain and often shifting meanings that attach to various terms that describe those who are thought to possess such powers. In other cases, of course, who gets called a magician, a sorcerer, or a witch can be a matter of life and death, depending on how severely a community or a court might judge such titles. Set against that backdrop, academic debates about the meanings of magic may not seem very consequential, but they are not completely removed from these other struggles either to define terms precisely or keep their implications somewhat vague. Throughout history, magic has been defined in part, and sometimes in large part, by outside observers rather than practitioners themselves. These include religious and legal authorities; intellectuals and academics; and also poets, playwrights, and other creators of myth and fiction.

Among academics, and especially between anthropologists, who tend to address magic and witchcraft around the world, and historians, who tend to focus mainly on Europe and North America, debates about labels and meanings often revolve around the use of what is called either emic or etic terminology.[29] That is, should scholars employ only the terms and concepts that exist to describe certain phenomena within the society they are studying (emic) or should they seek to apply terminology and categories derived from their own perspective (etic), which they regard to be more generalized and universal? While magic, sorcery, witchcraft, and so forth can all be considered emic terms within the context of Western history, they become etic ones when Western academics apply them to practices around the world, where they often confuse or obscure the meanings of native categories. But this is, in fact, only part of the problem. Even within Western history, terms for magic can become etic if a historian chooses to call a practice by a name that people of that time might not have used. For example, is it appropriate that I have called *goeteia* a kind of magic when it is not what the ancient Greeks would have (most often) called *mageia*? What if I were to insist, as a famous English historian once did, on referring to many of the rites and rituals of pre-Reformation Christianity as "the magic of the medieval church," when in fact medieval churchmen understood magic to be demonic and their own ceremonies to draw on divine power?[30]

One solution would be to abandon magic altogether as an academic category. We would then use the word "magic" only in those cases when specific historical actors have used it to describe their own practices or those that they have observed. In its place as a general category, we would devise different terminology to use when we wanted to discuss or compare practices across time and among different cultures. Unfortunately, this would not fully solve our problem either. As we have already seen, in many places around the world today, non-European people have readily adopted European terminology to describe their practices or to translate their native categories. Should we tell them they have no right? Likewise, should we tell a modern Wiccan living in Europe or North America that she shouldn't call her practices "witchcraft" because this is not what witchcraft meant five hundred years ago?

There is still another problem, though, which I consider to be even more serious. The use of completely clear and precisely defined etic categories to describe the world of magic, while undoubtedly useful in certain circumstances, would invariably tend to disguise the fact that the phenomenon we are studying and the emic terms that people have used to name it are themselves slippery, shifting, and inexact. *Mageia* and *goeteia* could sometimes mean the same or at least very similar things, just as *inyanga* and *sangoma* can sometimes be distinguished but other times are used interchangeably. In modern English, we would never call a practitioner of Wicca a "modern Sorcerer" instead of a modern Witch, but in other situations witchcraft and sorcery can mean essentially the same thing. This is not because people are misusing the terms in one case or the other but because these terms have meanings that shade into one another. In many cases, it is that shading of meaning that we want to capture.

In general, scholars like to work with clearly delineated analytical categories. But this is simply not possible, and, what's more, it is probably not entirely beneficial in the case of magic. As the anthropologist Peter Geschiere has observed, when the object of study can be understood in multiple ways from multiple perspectives, and when even native terminology used to describe it is either fluid or vague, then "the academic principle of clarity [may be] an obstacle rather than an asset."[31] Other scholars, particularly those working on magic in a comparative global context, are coming to this position as well. Adam Ashforth has noted how secrecy is central to conceptions of witchcraft, and to the power it manifests in society, in contemporary South Africa. Likewise, Roger Sansi and Luis Nicolau Parés, writing on "sorcery in the Black Atlantic," have described secrecy and concealment as essential components of magical systems. And drawing on their studies of magical and syncretic religions in the Caribbean, Diana Paton and Maarit Forde have observed that practitioners make no attempt to define themselves with clear and stable categories, so any attempts by academics to impose such categories on them are "fruitless."[32]

Regarding magic in Western European culture, the long dominance of historical studies focused on medieval and especially early modern witchcraft may have given us, scholars and students of this topic writ large, a false impression of how coherently a culture can view its own ideas of magic. Christian authorities, fervently condemning what they rigidly classified as demonic magic, appeared, for the most part, to agree on what they were writing about. Even if modern scholars thought their constructions to be largely fantastical, we still felt that they understood what they were describing in relatively coherent ways and that their views eventually came to be accepted by the majority of their society. Recent trends in scholarship, however, have led us to understand more about what ordinary people may have thought, believed, or feared. We have also begun to pay more attention to the uncertainties and open debates that existed among elite demonologists and other intellectual authorities. As we do so, we increasingly realize that even the notions of magic and witchcraft that sent so many thousands to the stake over the course of several centuries in Europe were never clear, stable, or completely agreed upon.

We may now be in a good position, therefore, to recognize that the problem of magic's convoluted meanings can become its own solution. Secrecy, uncertainty, and mysterious changeability are important hallmarks of magic around the world. These qualities are not diminished but are in fact highlighted when, in certain contexts, groups claiming particular insight or authority (including scholars) proclaim that they fully understand and can easily define magic. The uncertainties surrounding magic are different from the unknowns of science, and, I would suggest, from religious mysteries. In those cases, certain groups have the authority to set the parameters of the unknown and to fix the nature of the mystery. Magic is a debate between many voices. Regarding religious systems like modern neo-pagan Witchcraft or syncretic Vodou or Santería, which are proud of their lack of structural hierarchy and the crowdsourced development of their beliefs and practices, I hope this definition does not trample on their self-conception too much but instead helps to capture the sense in which they sometimes explicitly proclaim themselves to be magical.

In short, I would suggest that, whether in the modern age or throughout human history, when we find people engaging in rites or performing practices meant to invoke, sway, or control either natural or supernatural forces, but in ways that they may not fully understand themselves, or about which other segments of their society may have some very different understanding, we have probably found something that can be called magic. And when we find that the very words used to describe these rites and practices are shifting and elusive in their meanings, we may be doubly sure.

## NOTES

1 Voltaire, *Philosophical Dictionary*, trans. H. I. Wolff (New York: Knopf, 1924), entry on *Superstition*.
2 From Arthur C. Clarke, "Hazards of Prophecy: The Failure of Imagination," in *Profiles of the Future: An Enquiry into the Limits of the Possible* (New York: Harper and Row, 1962).
3 Theocritus, *Idylls* 2.
4 Exodus 7:8–24. Translation from the New Revised Standard Version.
5 1 Samuel 28:4–7.
6 Philip A. Kuhn, *Soulstealers: The Chinese Sorcery Scare of 1768* (Cambridge, MA: Harvard University Press, 1990), 105–11.
7 Fernando Cervantes, *The Devil in the New World: The Impact of Diabolism in New Spain* (New Haven, CT: Yale University Press, 1994), chap. 2.
8 Isidore of Seville, *Etymologies* 8.9.31, trans. Stephen A. Barney et al. (Cambridge: Cambridge University Press, 2006), 183.
9 Robert L. Park, *Superstition: Belief in the Age of Science* (Princeton, NJ: Princeton University Press, 2008), 215.
10 Pliny, *Natural History* 28.6.33, 28.7.35.
11 Gyan Prakash, "Between Science and Superstition: Religion and the Modern Subject of the Nation in Colonial India," in *Magic and Modernity: Interfaces of Revelation and Concealment*, ed. Birgit Meyer and Peter Pels (Stanford, CA: Stanford University Press, 2003), 39–59.
12 Stanley Jeyaraja Tambia, *Magic, Science, Religion, and the Scope of Rationality* (Cambridge: Cambridge University Press, 1990), 43, quoting R. R. Marett, who studied under Tylor.
13 Owen Davies, *Magic: A Very Short Introduction* (Oxford: Oxford University Press, 2012), 16.
14 Marcel Mauss, *A General Theory of Magic*, trans. Robert Brain (New York: Routledge, 2001), 28.
15 Emile Durkheim, *Elementary Forms of Religious Life*, trans. Karen E. Fields (New York: Free Press, 1995), 39–40.
16 Durkheim, *Elementary Forms*, 41, 42.
17 Bronislaw Malinowski, *Magic, Science and Religion, and Other Essays* (Glencoe, IL: Free Press, 1948), 86–87.
18 See Mary Douglas, "Thirty Years after *Witchcraft, Oracles and Magic*," in *Witchcraft Confessions and Accusations*, ed. Mary Douglas (1970; reprint New York: Routledge, 2004), xiii–xxxviii.

19 This divergence is summarized well at the outset of Ronald Hutton, "Anthropological and Historical Approaches to Witchcraft: Potential for a New Collaboration?" *The Historical Journal* 47 (2004): 413–34.

20 Sophocles, *Oedipus Tyrannus*, lines 385–96.

21 A good discussion is found in Kimberly B. Stratton, *Naming the Witch: Magic, Ideology, and Stereotype in the Ancient World* (New York: Columbia University Press, 2007), 6–11.

22 Quoted in Marco Pasi, "Varieties of Magical Experience: Aleister Crowley's Views on Occult Practice," in *Aleister Cowley and Western Esotericism*, ed. Henrik Bogdan and Martin P. Starr (Oxford: Oxford University Press, 2012), 66.

23 Helen A. Berger, "Witchcraft and Neopaganism," in *Witchcraft and Magic: Contemporary North America*, ed. Helen Berger (Philadelphia: University of Pennsylvania Press, 2005), 30.

24 Irene Silverblatt, *Moon, Sun, and Witches: Gender Ideologies and Class in Inca and Colonial Peru* (Princeton, NJ: Princeton University Press, 1987), 177–80.

25 Roger Sansi, "Sorcery and Fetishism in the Black Atlantic," in *Sorcery in the Black Atlantic*, ed. Luis Nicolau Parés and Roger Sansi (Chicago, IL: University of Chicago Press, 2011), 33.

26 Katherine Fidler, "Chiefs into Witches: Cosmopolitan Discourses of the Nation, Treason, and Sorcery; The Pondoland Revolt, South Africa," in *Sorcery in the Black Atlantic*, ed. Luis Nicolau Parés and Roger Sansi (Chicago, IL: The University of Chicago Press, 2011), 79–80.

27 Adam Ashforth, *Witchcraft, Violence, and Democracy in South Africa* (Chicago, IL: University of Chicago Press, 2005), 51–53.

28 Peter Geschiere, *Witchcraft, Intimacy, and Trust: Africa in Comparison* (Chicago, IL: University of Chicago Press, 2013), xviii, 3–5.

29 See e.g. the debate between Hildred Geertz, "An Anthropology of Religion and Magic I," and Keith Thomas, "An Anthropology of Religion and Magic II," *Journal of Interdisciplinary History* 6 (1975): 71–89, 91–109; although neither uses these terms directly.

30 Keith Thomas, *Religion and the Decline of Magic* (New York: Scribner's, 1971), chap. 2.

31 Peter Geschiere, "Witchcraft and Modernity: Perspectives from Africa and Beyond," in *Sorcery in the Black Atlantic*, ed. Luis Nicolau Parés and Roger Sansi (Chicago, IL: University of Chicago Press, 2010), 250.

32 Ashforth, *Witchcraft, Violence, and Democracy*, 14; Sansi and Parés's introduction to *Sorcery in the Black Atlantic*, 6–7; Maarit Forde and Diana Paton's introduction to *Obeah and Other Powers: The Politics of Caribbean Religion and Healing* (Durham, NC: Duke University Press, 2012), 8–9.

# 2

# MAGICAL ACTS

In what ways can magic be used? The possibilities are almost endless. Magic can win battles and predict the fate of nations. It can stir storms in the heavens and passions in the human heart. It has been used to heal as well as to harm, in some cases to kill, and in others to call the spirits of the dead back to earth. It can reveal secret information, such as the identity of a thief or murderer, the sex of an unborn child, or the location of some stolen sausages.[1] Some have used it to explore deep mysteries or attain higher levels of consciousness while others have sought to find buried treasure or to provide entertaining illusions for a fee. In short, magic can do whatever human beings can imagine, and the many ways in which it is performed can sometimes stagger the imagination. Magicians can wield wands, staffs, potions, or powders. They might employ herbs and roots, clumps of graveyard earth, special gems or inscribed images, body parts of animals, or even those of humans. Some perform elaborate rituals lasting days while others are thought to cast the evil eye with a passing glance.

There is no way to do justice to all the forms of magical practice that have existed in the past and that proliferate around the world today. My space is brief, but frankly, a longer account would still just be a catalog of endless variations. Here I will stick to broad categories, outlining various ways that people have cut up the magical pie. To put it more academically, I'll present various typologies of magic, which simply means that I'll group practices (and sometimes practitioners) together according to different characteristics. This is a favored approach among scholars, especially those who need to survey a broad topic. Of course, one can question how well the divisions drawn by academics line up with those used by people who believe themselves to have performed or experienced magic. Another real problem is that many magical practices don't fit neatly into just one category. Practitioners may use a spoken spell along with some natural ingredient such as an herb or special stone, which itself may have been gathered or otherwise prepared under a particular astral sign, and they may do this either to heal or to harm or in some cases to accomplish both at once.

There are no perfect ways around these problems, but I will try to resolve some of them by presenting several different typologies. First, I'll categorize magical practices according to the objectives they aim to achieve. Then I'll describe some basic ways in which magic can be performed, as well as different kinds of magical practitioners. Mainly I'll distinguish between practices available to anyone in a given society and kinds of magic used by people who are regarded in one way or another as specialists in their craft. I'll address more complicated issues of "magical identities," above all gender, but also foreignness and racial or ethnic identities, in a later chapter. Here, I'll continue by surveying various items or materials that magicians might use, and I'll conclude with a consideration of the different sources of power on which various kinds of magical practices are believed to draw.

## THE USES OF MAGIC

Without a doubt, the most prevalent use of magic across time has been to heal. For example, scholars have identified a simple spell against toothaches among the many rites of ancient Mesopotamian magic.[2] In most early human societies, in fact, forms of magic intertwined with medical practices so completely as to be virtually indistinguishable to many later observers. Yet also from antiquity onwards, physicians have vehemently tried to distinguish their field of expertise from that of magicians. The ancient Greek treatise *On the Sacred Disease*, written around 400 BCE and attributed to Hippocrates, the father of Western medicine, ridiculed magicians as fools or charlatans, and around 400 CE the early Christian authority Augustine of Hippo included in his general condemnation of magical and superstitious practice "all amulets and healing charms that medical science condemns."[3]

Despite such rhetoric, healing magic remained in use. One of the best known magical amulets in medieval Europe invoked the biblical Three Kings to relieve epilepsy, and around the year 1300, Pope Boniface VIII commissioned the Catalan physician, astrologer, and alchemist Arnau of Vilanova to treat his kidney stones, which Arnau did through a golden astrological talisman.[4] A century later, the theologian Jean Gerson, chancellor of the University of Paris, chastised his own medical faculty for condoning amulets and other magical remedies that were normally used only by fraudulent magicians and "old women sorceresses." He subsequently wrote a short tract dedicated exclusively to condemning an astrological talisman of exactly the sort that Arnau of Vilanova has used to treat Boniface VIII, this time having been fashioned by the dean of the prominent medieval medical school in Montpellier.[5]

It is fascinating to compare Gerson's rhetoric to that of the South African physician and political leader Nthato Motlana more than five hundred years later. Addressing the graduating class of medical students at the University of Witwatersrand in 1976, he decried traditional forms of African healing as magical superstition. He especially criticized the increased respectability that these practices had recently attained, even among medical professionals, and he denounced the World Health Organization's advocacy that more official recognition should be given to traditional healers. While he recognized that some traditional practices might have a sound scientific basis, Moltana characterized most of them as ineffective and fraudulent.[6]

Despite similar efforts to castigate them as charlatans, self-styled *curanderos* (healers) continue to practice widely in Latin America, and *botánicas*, shops stocked with medicinal herbs and other paraphernalia for the practice of Santería and other Afro-Caribbean religions, can be found in many major North American cities as well. Traditional healers have also practiced in Europe into modern times, whether they call themselves *curanderos* (Spain), *curatori* (Italy), or cunning-folk (England). People tend to seek magical cures especially when they feel that they have suffered magical harm, so these healers often, although by no means always, specialize in undoing bewitchments. This connection, too, has an ancient past. An herbal remedy against witchcraft from ancient Mesopotamia involved giving the sufferer ingredients mixed in "first-rate beer" while facing into the sunrise on the last day of the month and speaking a certain incantation.[7]

Magical harm is closely linked to magical healing, and across the world people have long been accused of causing illness, injury, and death by magical means. Often these people are thought of as malevolent witches who are evil to their core, but other more ordinary folk can also turn to harmful magic in particular situations. So-called curse tablets, which were widespread in the Greco-Roman world, could be used to strike out at enemies in many ways, including weakening competitors in athletic contests or, especially among the litigious ancient Athenians, binding the tongues or dulling the wits of opponents in court proceedings.[8] From the ancient West to Han China, poisoning and other forms of harmful magic were used to eliminate political rivals.[9] In medieval Europe, Benedictine monks would ritually curse anyone who harmed them or their monasteries' tenants, although they would not, of course, have thought of what they were doing as performing harmful magic but rather calling down just divine retribution.

Aside from healing or harming in specific ways, magic can also provide all-encompassing protection. The Mesopotamian *Maqlû* ceremony, mentioned in the Introduction, was meant as a sweeping defense against harmful magic, and many magical amulets have been intended to ensure general wellbeing, right down to today's lucky rabbit's foot. People have sought to avoid harm or misfortune by wearing such special items, or by visiting special places such as temple sites, by performing certain ritual actions (have you ever thrown salt over your shoulder or knocked on wood?), or by avoiding some taboo (don't walk under a ladder). In modern China, some people believe that eating expensive foods such as dumplings filled with meat or pine seeds will help avert general misfortune.[10] Other rites aim to protect against more specific forms of harm, or to shield specific kinds of people. Rites to help mothers during pregnancy and childbirth are found around the world. Likewise, magic is frequently employed to protect men in warfare. In Greek myth, or at least in one version of it, the mother of the hero Achilles dipped him in the river Styx to make him invulnerable.[11] Both Boxer militias in China and Zulu warriors in southern Africa claimed magical invulnerability against bullets and other weapons when battling European powers in the late nineteenth and early twentieth centuries, and an American anthropologist who apprenticed as a sorcerer in modern Niger was once presented with a magical powder that could protect him from "guns, bullets, accidents, and evil people."[12]

Especially in premodern, predominantly agricultural societies, the fertility of crops and livestock has been essential and often precarious. Drought, disease, insects, or heavy storms could prove devastating. In addition to arising naturally, all were potentially thought to be caused by magical means, and so societies the world over has developed innumerable protective rites. In medieval and early modern Europe, peasants rang church bells to avert impending storms and erected crosses in the fields to provide general protection. Priests could process through the fields with consecrated Eucharist wafers, and bishops might sometimes formally exorcise fields of insects and vermin.[13] Similarly, in China even into the Communist era peasants might burn incense to bring rain to drought-stricken crops or to drive away locusts.[14]

Another enormous field of magic is divination. Think about all the things you would like to know but don't. Divination often involves seeing into the future, and in many societies, it borders uneasily on what is usually framed as the more religious practice of prophecy. In the biblical account of the Hebrew King Saul and the "witch" of Endor, Saul consults a medium to learn the outcome of an impending battle with the Philistines only after God fails to reveal it to him through either prophets' dreams or *Urim*.[15] This last practice, along with *Thummim*, refers to a priestly divination employed in ancient Hebrew society (but still not fully understood by scholars). In many other societies, diviners have likewise been thought to summon spirits, either supernatural beings or souls of the human dead, to relate the future. Other common divinatory practices have scientific rather than religious overtones. Horoscopes and other kinds of astrological prognostications have been rooted in scientific and philosophical traditions from the ancient West through India and into China. Ancient Mayan astrology made news in 2012 when some people believed that it predicted the end of the world would occur. Throughout history, political leaders have relied on astrologers to guide their actions. After the attempted assassination of U.S. President Ronald Reagan in 1981, First Lady Nancy Reagan regularly consulted the astrologer Joan

Quigley to try to foresee and avoid other dangers during the rest of his presidency.

Many other forms of divination are common across cultures, such as casting lots (known as *sortilegium* to the ancient Romans, and, as we saw in the previous chapter, the root of the later English word "sorcery"). Many societies have also had forms of bibliomancy, which involves using passages randomly chosen from books thought to contain special truth in order to peer into the future. Medieval Christians used the Bible (but also Virgil's *Aeneid*) and Muslims the Qur'an, while the Chinese have used the *I Ching*. There are also innumerable more passive forms of divination involving signs or omens. The ancient Romans, for example, developed augury, based on observing the flight of birds, into a complex art. Animals of almost any kind can be regarded as omens, either through their actions or just by encountering them. In many parts of the modern world, people take a black cat crossing their path as a bad sign, for example. Even in aggressively modernizing and officially atheistic Communist China, rumors of talking toads or other portentous animals, or encounters with ghosts or spirits can provoke widespread concern about impending misfortune or disaster.[16]

Aside from gaining knowledge about the future in some way, divination can also be used to reveal other kinds of hidden information. In the world prior to sonograms, for example, many traditional practices existed that would supposedly reveal the sex of a baby still in the womb. Practices also existed to find lost or stolen items, or to identify thieves, murderers, or other criminals. The identification of witches, who in many societies have been both the worst and most secret malefactors, has often been an important function of divination. In certain modern African courts, accusations of witchcraft must be confirmed by a traditional healer, who helped to detect the harmful magic, to be accepted.[17]

Other kinds of rites, usually not thought of specifically as divination, purport to be able to confer heightened knowledge, wisdom, or understanding of either human sciences or the mysteries of the universe. In medieval Europe, the so-called *ars notoria*, or notary art (named after the ritual figures, *notae*, in its texts), consisted of rites sometimes ascribed to Solomon that were intended to conjure angelic spirits that would then confer knowledge on the practitioner. Other theurgic rites, such as those associated with

Jewish Kabbalah, aimed at spiritual elevation or the attainment of mystical wisdom. In the modern era, Western occultists, who frequently see themselves as drawing on ancient wisdom and reviving ancient rites, but who are also deeply informed by modern psychology, have developed rituals intended to alter or expand the practitioner's consciousness.

Beyond altering one's own psyche, magic has often aimed to alter or control the psyches of others. Love magic abounds. Across almost all cultures and throughout history people have employed rites or concocted potions that they think will inspire love or just inflame passion in someone else, or conversely that might sow discord between lovers or enmity between friends. Other forms of erotic magic aim for physical effects, causing impotence or infertility, or curing these afflictions, promoting reproduction, or serving as a contraceptive or abortifacient. As already mentioned, most traditional cultures have an array of practices intended to help pregnant women and promote healthy childbirth. Many also have rites intended to keep husbands from straying, either rekindling their passion for their wives or in some physical way preventing them from copulating outside of the marriage bed.

For as long as humans have been driven by ambitions for wealth and success, magical practices have existed to help obtain these goals. In the classical West, merchants and artisans inscribed curses on small lead tablets to gain an advantage over competitors. One, for example, invokes the "Goddess of Vengeance" to "cause the entire business in which Manes [presumably a rival] is engaged to become entirely contrary and backward."[18] In central Europe, a spell invoking the new moon to grant wealth has existed since at least the Middle Ages.[19] In modern Cameroon a quite recent form of witchcraft called *nyongo* centers around generating wealth. Rather than simply killing their victims, these witches supposedly make them into zombies known as *vekongi*, who then labor for the witches on "invisible plantations" that produce occult wealth.[20] Similarly, *Feymen* are conmen who make money through counterfeiting, rigged gambling, shady dealing in secondhand goods, and other kinds of financial swindling. The unclear nature of their dealings has caused many people to associate them with magical practices, to the extent that their money itself can be regarded as bewitched and a source of infection to others.[21]

Another major purpose of magic is to perform marvelous feats, particularly in terms of transportation and transformation. What image of witchcraft is more ubiquitous, at least in Western societies, than a witch flying on a broomstick, and what image is more indicative of Middle Eastern magic than a flying carpet? Hindu holy men are often depicted being able to levitate, as are many Christian saints. In modern Africa witches have updated their mode of flight and now are often thought to use invisible airplanes. Throughout history magicians have also been depicted changing their shape or the shape of other things. In Book Ten of Homer's *Odyssey*, Circe transforms Odysseus's men into swine, while in the biblical Book of Exodus, Aaron's rod transforms into a snake before Pharaoh, and then Egyptian magicians match this with transformations of their own.

Perhaps because of their potentially showy nature, these sorts of feats have often been thought to be illusory in some way, even by people who otherwise believe fully in the reality of magic. For example, while medieval and early modern Christian doctrine proclaimed that demons absolutely could transport witches (or anyone else, for that matter) bodily through the air, many authorities held that witches typically traveled to their nighttime sabbaths only in spirit-form, something that scholars have subsequently compared to the spirit-journeys undertaken by shamans in many cultures. Physical transformations, too, have been argued to be tricks or illusions rather than real metamorphoses.

In fact, creating illusions is a significant purpose of magic in its own right. These can be malevolent or harmful. The famous European witch-hunting manual *Malleus Maleficarum* maintains that witches would often steal penises (a rather graphic form of impotence-magic), apparently removing them from men's bodies and stashing them in crates or even hiding them in birds' nests in trees. The *Malleus* assured its readers, however, that all this was only a vile illusion and that in fact male members remained firmly attached to their bodies.[22] Other forms of magical misdirection could be far more benign, akin to modern stage magic. Another medieval European text, a notebook kept by a monk named Thomas Betson, describes how to attach a fine strand of hair to a coin and so cause it to appear to move on its own, or how one could put a beetle inside a hollowed-out apple to make it rock back and forth seemingly of its own accord.[23] These tricks were not meant to terrify but to entertain and delight, which has always been another major purpose for which people have turned to magic throughout the ages.

## PRACTICES AND PRACTITIONERS

Forms of magical practice vary as widely as the purposes to which they can be put. Many people distinguish broadly between white and black magic, that is, between magic used in beneficial or harmful ways. Some maintain that these categories involve entirely different kinds of practices, but as we've seen harmful forms of magic are often just the inverse of helpful ones, and quite frequently the very same people are thought to be able to do both. Other kinds of magic do not fit this dichotomy at all. A love spell, for example, would be beneficial for the person who gains a desired lover but would have to be thought of as harmful to the person who is compelled to love someone for whom he or she would not otherwise feel affection. A more useful but still very basic dichotomy among magical practices can be drawn between what is often called high and low magic. High magic is complex, typically involving long and detailed rites. It also tends to involve more sophisticated, often expensive, paraphernalia (which will be discussed more in the next section of this chapter) such as precious metals or gemstones, polished mirrors, or carefully crafted images. Low magic, by contrast, involves simpler rites such as brief spoken spells or relatively limited ritual actions. Its material components, if any are necessary, are usually common plants, stones, or basic household items.

While practitioners of high magic frequently present it as a refined art or even a form of science that requires long study, practitioners of low magic achieve their expertise, and stake their claims to power, in other ways, and some kinds of low magic require no special expertise at all. While high magic, at least in most societies, is the domain of certain specialized elites, low magic can be practiced by people further down their society's social scale. Here too, we need to be careful about drawing any absolute distinction, because in many cultures very highly placed people can also perform relatively basic, common forms of magic. Nevertheless, these distinctions show that different kinds of magical practices often relate directly to the different kinds of people who practice them. While it is a tautology, for example, to state that witchcraft is performed by witches, this is exactly the distinction that people have sometimes drawn between witchcraft and other forms of magical practice. *Malleus Maleficarum*, for example, warns that people who have been bewitched should not turn to other witches for a remedy or cure. It then separately condemns, somewhat less harshly, magical cures that involve the same "witch-like rites" (*maleficiales ritus*) but that are not performed by a person identified as a witch.[24] And let us not forget, of course, that "magic" itself originally meant practices performed by Persian *magoi*.

The most basic types of magical practices in any society are not reserved for specialists at all but are available essentially to everyone. Have you ever used a Ouija board or a deck of tarot cards? Then you have engaged in divination and possibly spirit conjuration. Perhaps you didn't take your actions very seriously, but people in many cultures turn to magic at least in part as a diversion or entertainment, although these lines can quickly shift. The grim events of the Salem witch trials in seventeenth-century Massachusetts began with a group of young girls playing a game to divine "what trade their [future] sweethearts should be of." They did so by dropping an egg white into a glass of water, and they became terrified when it seemed to take the shape of a coffin.[25] Have you ever bent down to pick up a penny because it is good luck to do so? Adjusting for inflation, the thirteenth-century French theologian William of Auvergne castigated people who believed that finding a halfpenny brought good luck, which he considered to be a dangerous superstition.[26]

Such practices are performed rather whimsically in modern Western societies, because modern Western culture, or at least the dominant culture in the modern West, does not take magic very seriously. In other societies, however, even relatively simple and ordinary magical practices carry more weight. In medieval Europe, for example, people would write the Lord's Prayer on a slip of paper or other material, or they would find someone who could write it for them, and place this on a sick person. Many no doubt saw this action as a legitimate religious practice, akin to praying for a sick person's health, and some church authorities even agreed. Others, however, were suspicious of what they saw as a potentially improper and illicit rite.[27] A slightly more elaborate ritual involved writing the opening words of the *Pater noster* on sage leaves and feeding these to a sick person three mornings in a row. This would supposedly cure fever.[28] Into the nineteenth and even the twentieth centuries, French peasants still recited simple prayers/incantations to heal injury and illness, such as this against burns: "Fire, lose your heat, as Judas lost his color in the Garden of Olives."[29]

In many cases, people probably performed these actions without even thinking about whether they were magical or not, just as some people might turn to the horoscopes in a modern newspaper without pausing to reflect that they are about to partake in a form of astrological divination. In other cases, however, we know that people worried a great deal about the nature of the practices in which they engaged. In late-medieval Germany, a woman from a small town along the Rhine knew an incantation that she thought would help heal her injured son, but she feared to use it because her local clergyman told her that it was an illicit spell rather than an approved benediction. Instead, she sought out other clergymen, until she found one in a town a few miles away who told her that the rite she wanted to perform was perfectly fine. This clergyman, whose name was Werner of Friedberg, also knew a healing incantation of his own: "Christ was born, Christ was lost, Christ was found again; may he bless these wounds in the name of the Father, and of the Son, and of the Holy Spirit." He thought this spell was probably superstitious, but he still used it himself – until he was put on trial for his unorthodox ideas.[30] Similarly, the seventeenth-century Chinese writer Wang Bu presents himself as skeptical about magical practices, but when he encountered an evil spirit "with two eyes like mirrors," he relates that he quickly recited the traditional protective "Spell of Tianpeng," causing it to flee. Chinese people still used the Spell of Tianpeng into the modern period, as well as inscribing protective magical characters on the doors to their houses, and using the *I Ching*, thought to have protective powers, to ward off evil spirits.[31]

The examples of Werner of Friedberg and Wang Bu show that educated elites are just as capable of using the simple rites that might be described as low magic as anyone else in their societies. It is also important to realize that some common rites can be reasonably elaborate. Returning to medieval Europe, peasants might seek to protect their fields from storms and especially from hail by declaring "I adjure you, hail and winds, by the three holy nails of Christ, which pierced the hands and feet of Christ, and by the four evangelists, saints Matthew, Mark, Luke, and John, that you come down dissolved into water," or they might simply set up crosses in their fields. They could also, however, take four pieces of a specific wood, namely oak, and fashion a cross that they would face in the direction of the coming storm and light on fire so that the storm would change its course away from this protective beacon. Even more elaborately, they could set up a cross in a field, light a fire, and throw hailstones they had collected into the fire while invoking the Trinity, then reciting the Lord's Prayer three times, then the Hail Mary, then the opening words of the Gospel of John, all while making the sign of the cross in each of the four cardinal directions.[32] Whether people at the time would have considered this a magical rite or not (church authorities clearly did), they would almost certainly not have thought of those who performed the rite as specialist magicians. They were just ordinary farmers going about the business of protecting their crops.

Far removed from such ordinary people who sometimes turned to magic would be highly educated ritual experts who specialized in very complex and elaborate rites, usually following some written formula. The ceremony known as *Maqlû*, performed by priests in ancient Mesopotamia to ward off evil spirits and to protect against harmful magic, covers eight tablets, contains over one hundred separate incantations, and would last an entire night. Many millennia later, the theological faculty of the medieval University of Paris described and condemned a detailed ritual in which a group of magicians, all stripped to the waist and holding polished swords, gathered around a "great circle conscribed with divers unknown names and marked with various characters." They placed a raised wheel within this circle and set a bottle on the wheel, which they then covered with a scroll containing yet more signs, symbols, and strange names. They lit a fire, burned incense, and read out incantations. All this was to conjure a spirit that would reveal the location of some hidden treasure.[33]

In the nineteenth century, one of the leading figures of modern occultism, Éliphas Lévi, described how to fashion a ritual pentagram. It should be made of seven different metals, or "at least" of pure gold set in marble, or traced in vermilion on an "unblemished" lambskin taken from a lamb slaughtered during the Pascal season with a new knife and preserved with consecrated salt. The pentagram itself should be consecrated with holy water, suffumigated with various perfumes, then "breathed on" five times while the magician invoked five different angels. After yet further ceremonies and rituals, the finished pentagram would exert "a great influence on spirits" of all kinds. Lévi stressed that the "omission of even one of these difficult and apparently arbitrary ceremonies makes void the entire success of the great works of science."[34] The complexity and obscurity of these rites are part of their power. Likewise, the ritual magician gains his aura of power (or sometimes her aura, but in most societies these experts have more often been men than women) through long study to gain arcane knowledge.

Many magical specialists lack the secret learning and the (often self-proclaimed) intellectual pedigrees possessed by practitioners of elite ritual conjurations, and the magic they perform may be more like the basic rites available to anyone in their society, but they still claim special expertise or abilities. Such people are often called cunning-men or cunning-women, but they are also known as healers, diviners, witch-doctors, and a myriad of other terms. Witches, too, would be counted among this type of magical practitioner, for they are typically seen as otherwise ordinary people who have access to special (often nefarious) powers.

These people sometimes base their claim to power in the same way as elite ritual magicians do, that is, through study and possession of esoteric knowledge. Such knowledge can even be transmitted through texts, albeit usually less elaborate ones than those elite magicians possess or claim to know. In Europe, especially after the advent of printing greatly increased the availability of inexpensive texts in vernacular languages, many cunning-folk had access to magical books. Even if they could not read themselves, just possessing a magical text could confer an aura of authority to their actions, but many could read, and there is even evidence that some kept written records of their own practices. In the seventeenth and eighteenth centuries, cheap printed chapbooks known in France as *Bibliotheque bleue* included many magical texts, which circulated by the thousands. They also penetrated the French-speaking regions of the Caribbean, contributing to the syncretic mix that would feed into Vodou and similar practices in the New World. In many parts of Africa, on the other hand, even after European powers achieved colonial domination, traditional healers and diviners were more likely to rely on Arabic magical texts. The thirteenth-century *Shams al-ma'ārif* (Illumination of Knowledge), for example, has been printed in the modern period from North Africa to India.[35]

Of course, book-learning is not the only way people can gain access to special knowledge. Magical specialists might claim that their skills have been handed down through oral traditions, perhaps within their family or through a lineage of masters and pupils. Often there is something about specialists themselves that sets them apart, and their claims to power involve some aspect of their person. Among the Maka in Cameroon, the magical essence *djambe* is either inherited, by boys from their fathers and by girls from their mothers, or old people can pass their *djambe* to infants by blowing in their mouths.[36] In early modern Italy, so-called *benandanti* (literally, "those who go well") were marked by being born with the caul, a piece of the amniotic membrane still covering all or part of the head. They were then widely believed to engage in spirit-journeys, battle witches, and have special power as healers. Sometimes such marking can come later in life. In Bali, for example, strange bodily signs, such as hair suddenly growing in a mass that cannot be untangled, or finding special objects, such as a gem inside a rice cake, indicated that certain people had been "called" by the gods. They were then thought to have special power, although often only for a brief period.[37] *Brujos* (witch-healers) in modern Puerto Rico may identify themselves as having been called to this practice by a vision of a Catholic saint or the Virgin Mary. In the African-American "conjure" tradition, people may learn skills from other practitioners, but they can also be marked at birth (such as by the caul), or they may feel themselves to have been called spiritually, akin to the Christian notion of feeling a call to the ministry.[38]

People regarded by their neighbors as malevolent witches may be thought to possess special knowledge, particularly if they are believed to work their witchcraft through potions, powders, or other natural materials. As we've seen, in many cultures the words for poison or poisoning can also designate witchcraft. But witches are also often marked in their persons. In one of the most graphic depictions of a witch in Western antiquity, the Roman poet Lucan described how the terrible Erictho worked with spells and poisons, but also how crops withered at her step and how her breath turned the air poisonous, as if evil and corruption simply oozed out of her.[39] In Africa, the Azande people, famously studied by anthropologist E. E. Evans-Pritchard, regarded witchcraft as a substance within a person, like the Maka mentioned above. But Azande witches did not necessarily know that they had this power. It could act independently of them, and some people performed rites to try to stifle the power of witchcraft if they suspected it resided within them.[40] A very personalized and in fact embodied force thereby became a general and amorphous threat.

Witchcraft, as it was conceived in Europe during the period of the major witch trials from the fifteenth through the eighteenth centuries, presents significant contrasts but also interesting parallels to Azande notions. Official Christian demonology insisted that witches possessed no special powers themselves. They gained their ability to perform witchcraft only by entering pacts with demons. It was these evil spirits who taught witches to brew poisons or simply performed harmful magic directly at their behest. Nevertheless, there are many indications in popular accounts, and sometimes in the writings of demonologists themselves, that witchcraft was thought to be passed down within families, or that older witches taught younger ones their craft. Thus, witchcraft could both be located within particular people and also represent evil on a vast, cosmic scale.

## MAGICAL MATERIALS

While some kinds of magic may simply radiate out from certain specially empowered individuals, most magic involves actions. And while these actions may involve formulaic words or ritual gestures, very often material implements are also used. Such magical materials can exist in nature, or they can be specially manufactured through magical rites. They may be regarded as possessing power inherently, as having power imbued into them, or as focusing and directing outside energies. Just as there are elite forms of magic that require considerable time and training to perform, so there are elite magical items that take great effort or expense to acquire: gems, precious metals, rare spices, exotic plants, or body parts of exotic animals. Other items can be considered elite because of the time and skill needed to create them: complex astrological talismans (often crafted from precious materials), altars, statues or figures, or detailed images, drawings, or geometric forms that purport to draw on deep esoteric knowledge. Magic circles are common in many Western forms of ritual conjuration, and magic squares, usually replete with astrological or other mystical symbols, probably originated in China and spread westward.

Among the most ubiquitous magical materials are in fact books or other texts intended to impart knowledge of magical practices and in some cases also regarded as powerful objects. They are often rare texts circulating only within certain elite groups. And, of course, in societies where literacy is not common, all texts are rare and restricted. In that situation, writing itself can be an esoteric, powerful, and often magical act. But as we've also seen already, some forms of magical texts can circulate quite widely and have considerable popular appeal.

Much of our knowledge of magic in antiquity is necessarily based on a few surviving texts. Clay tablets containing spells and other rites, such as the *Maqlû* ritual that I have described several times already or the equally intricate *Šurpu* ceremony, have been unearthed in Mesopotamia. A remarkable treasure-trove of documents known as the Greek Magical Papyri details rites from Greco-Roman Egypt in the second through fifth centuries CE. The papyri circulated secretly and were only rediscovered in the nineteenth century by an antiquities collector in Cairo, who gathered many texts together and sold them to various European libraries.[41] The *Sepher ha-Razim*, a Jewish mystical and magical text likely from the third or fourth century CE, was only identified in 1963 by a scholar working in a collection that had come from Cairo to Oxford University.[42] Throughout the Middle Ages, in both Christian Europe and the Islamic world, magical texts drew, or at least claimed to draw, on ancient sources but also incorporated new forms of magic. Often these texts crossed cultural boundaries. The Arabic *Ghāyat al-Ḥakīm* (Aim of the Wise) is a manual of mostly astral magic, drawing on the power of the stars but also on spirits that could be invoked and controlled. It was written, probably in the eleventh century, and entered Europe in the thirteenth century, when it was translated first into Spanish on the order of King Alphonso X of Castile and then into Latin as *Picatrix*.

Along with astrology and astral magic, alchemy is another elite, text-driven form of magic. The most famous alchemical text in the Western tradition, the so-called Emerald Tablet, is just one paragraph long, and traditionally, attributed to the legendary Hermes Trismegistus, or Thrice-Great Hermes. This mythical figure gave his name to an entire body of mystical and magical writings, the Hermetic corpus, which originated mainly from the first through fourth centuries CE. The Emerald Tablet, however, is probably from the eighth century, with the earliest known version being appended to the ninth-century Arabic *Kitāb Sirr al-Khalīqa* (Book of the Secret of Creation).[43] Numerous other alchemical texts are attributed to the Muslim scholar Jābir ibn-Ḥayyān, who lived supposedly from the early 700s to the early 800s. In fact, the works attributed to him probably represent a whole school of Arab and Persian alchemists.

Arabic and Persian texts traveled east as well as west, circulating through India and southeast Asia. South Asia of course also had its own tradition of magical and ritual texts. The Atharvaveda, for example, is one of the four Vedas, the sacred texts of Hinduism. Written in Sanskrit and dating to the second millennium BCE, sections of it contain spells, incantations, and healing charms. Powerful ritual texts in Bali are written in Kawi, that is, Old Javanese.[44] In the modern era, Western occultists have eagerly appropriated Eastern systems (real or imagined) into their magical rites and their own magical texts. As we've seen in the previous section, Arabic texts continue to circulate in the Middle East and across much of Africa, while European grimoires have made their way to North and South America. For some practitioners of modern Witchcraft, so-called Books of Shadows are important repositories of spells and rituals. Even the entirely fictional *Necronomicon*, invented by the early-twentieth-century horror write H. P. Lovecraft and attributed by him to "the mad Arab Abdul Alhazred," now exists in several versions, composed entirely post-facto by fans of Lovecraft's work. The varieties of magical texts are vast indeed.

Another ubiquitous magical item is the amulet. Small objects worn or carried typically for protective purposes have been evident in human cultures since time immemorial. In antiquity, the eye of the Egyptian god Horus etched into a medallion was thought to ward off harm and was used not just in Egypt but across the Near

East. A palm-shaped amulet known as the hamsa, which often contains an eye and has its roots in antiquity, is still popular across the Middle East and North Africa. Also known in Islamic regions as the Hand of Fatima (the daughter of the Prophet Muhammad), it is thought to protect against the evil eye. In West Africa, Muslim marabouts frequently combine various materials into protective amulets. In the sixteenth century, Portuguese traders began to wear what they called mandinga pouches, because they were originally fashioned by marabouts of the Mandinka people. These spread across the Atlantic world; they were used by blacks and whites, masters and slaves; and by the eighteenth century they had become prevalent even in the imperial metropole of Lisbon. In the southern United States, as well, slaves relied on amulets for protection from the endless hardships in their lives. These could be crafted figures, but they were often bags of materials. Typical contents could include graveyard earth, a rabbit's foot, or a bone from a black cat.[45]

Wands and staffs have an equally long history as magical objects, being used to focus or direct power. Rather than the slender magician's wand familiar today from stage shows or *Harry Potter* movies, or a full-sized wizard's staff, these were more often intermediate-sized rods, likely based on the scepters that served as symbols of rulership for monarchs in many cultures. In Homer's *Odyssey*, Circe transforms Odysseus's men into swine with such a rod (*rhados* in Greek). When Moses and Aaron confront Pharaoh to demand the release of the Hebrews from slavery in the biblical Book of Exodus the first wonder they perform is for Aaron to throw down his rod (also *rhados* in the Greek Septuagint) and have it transform into a serpent. More commonplace kinds of staffs and sticks have also long been thought to serve other magical purposes. Probably no image of Western European witchcraft is more famous than that of witches riding broomsticks, although especially in German-speaking lands during the height of the early modern witch trials they were even more commonly thought to ride on simple cooking forks, the large sticks used in kitchens to hold items over a fire. In modern Witchcraft today, both wands and broomsticks can be employed as ritual objects.

Flat, reflective surfaces seem to cry out for images to fill them, and long before the era of the TV screen or computer monitor, such surfaces were used to conjure visions and perceive far-away events. The art of scrying, as efforts to summon such visions are called, can use almost any surface, the most basic being a pool of reflective water. The twelfth-century English clergyman John of Salisbury wrote that when he was a schoolboy his teacher anointed his fingernail with oil and tried to conjure demonic images in it. Other sources indicate that medieval magicians might similarly use a crystal, a mirror, the blade of a sword, of even the "greased shoulder-blade of a ram."[46] In the sixteenth century, the famous English mage John Dee settled on using crystals in which he tried to conjure visions of angels. Eventually this developed into the modern crystal-gazing of nineteenth- and twentieth-century occultists (although crystal balls per se probably derived initially from stage shows, not real efforts at divination).

The list of items crafted for or later co-opted into magical use could be extended indefinitely: magic rings, magic mirrors, magic cloaks, magic shoes, magic lamps, magic carpets, magic bags, and magic closets, to say nothing of magically empowered weapons of every conceivable kind. But equally endless is the list of magical materials simply found in nature. Many herbs, roots, flowers, or other kinds of plants have been thought to possess magical properties. Sometimes their powerful characteristics are always available for use, while other times they need to have their magic activated, so to speak, by being gathered under special circumstances, such as during a full moon, or just before dawn at mid-summer. Obviously, many plants have natural medicinal qualities, and others are poisonous. One of the most magically charged plants of all time is surely the mandrake, the root of which many people think resembles a human being. A member of the nightshade family, the mandrake contains hallucinogenic chemicals and can be poisonous. The Roman naturalist, Pliny the Elder, noted that mandrake could be fatal but taken in the right quantities it was useful in treating eye diseases.[47] Others thought it could make a powerful love potion. The legend that the plant was so powerful that it would kill anyone who uprooted it goes back at least to the first-century CE Jewish historian Josephus, although only later works presented the solution. One should tie a leash to a dog and fasten the other end to the mandrake. Then, from a safe distance, one could call the dog and it would pull the plant from the ground, thereby suffering death in its master's stead.[48]

Around the world, all sorts of natural materials have been put to magical use. In Zambia, *nsomu* is a powerful agent made from the inner nerve of a recently killed elephant's right tusk, combined with reed salt, and then used in divination. In South Africa, *muthi* is a generic term for magical material made from many substances and used for many purposes. It can protect a person or a place, but it can also be used to harm someone or to gain wealth. Perhaps the most terrible *muthi* is made from body parts of people deliberately murdered to provide magical ingredients.[49] Human remains have a gruesome history of use in magic. Witches from antiquity onwards have been thought to haunt graveyards, to dig up corpses, and to pull the bodies of executed criminals down from crosses, gibbets, and gallows. Many kinds of animals or animal parts also figure in magical practices. Venomous creatures have served to make magical potions and poisons from antiquity to the present, and from Western Europe to the Far East, but other kinds of animals are used for other purposes as well. Doves, for example, are often associated with purity and other positive qualities, while hoopoes have frequently been considered to be very efficacious for summoning and controlling demons.

Not content to rely on natural properties alone, magicians often combine natural materials with invocations and conjurations, the power of spirits, or that of astral bodies. Modern Puerto Rican *brujos*, for example, frequently work with herbs, oils, and powders. But they also employ these elements in ceremonies performed on altars, with lighted candles, and other ritual actions. In a similar but far more gruesome vein, a magical handbook from fifteenth-century Europe presents a particularly multifaceted love spell. A conjurer should first obtain a completely white dove and parchment made from a female dog skinned while in heat. This is because "this kind of parchment is most powerful for gaining the love of a woman." He should then tear out the dove's heart with his teeth and, using a quill made from an eagle's feather, draw an image of a naked woman with its blood on the parchment. He must then write the names of various demons on the image while invoking them, and then burn myrrh and saffron while performing more conjurations over the image. Having done all this, the object of his desire is sure to fall in love with him. Even if she is far away, the demons will be able to bring her to him if he inscribes a circle in the earth and performs yet more conjurations while gazing at a magic ring. When the woman appears, "she will be a bit astonished," but the magician need only touch her with the parchment on which he has drawn her image and she will be enraptured with him. The text helpfully advises that "it is better to make the circle as large as possible," so that the magician and his lover can lie down comfortably within it.[50]

## SOURCES OF MAGICAL POWER

As the example above shows, magical rites often combine numerous elements and appear to draw on a range of powers. The most basic distinction that can be drawn here is between spiritual and natural forces. Scholars sometimes categorize various kinds of magic in this way, but it has also been an important distinction, in certain contexts, for practitioners of magic to try to make themselves. To claim that the magic one performs relies on entirely natural forces can be a way to defend oneself from condemnation. Properties or powers that exist in nature are often regarded, at least in many societies, and being morally neutral. They may be used for harmful purposes, but they are not evil in themselves, and neither are the people who know how to use them, at least not automatically so. Claiming that one has summoned spiritual forces or being accused of this can complicate matters. While some cultures believe in morally neutral spirits, in many belief systems spiritual beings are either good or bad. Thus even if a magician claims to be acting in a good cause, perhaps to heal or protect someone from harm, he or she might still face condemnation for having engaged with evil forces to do so.

The distinction between spiritual and natural magic has been particularly important in Western history, because Christianity, which has shaped Western societies for the past two millennia for both Christians and non-Christians alike, draws an extremely sharp moral division between the spiritual powers it believes exist in the universe. On one side are God and his angels while on the other are the devil and all the demons of hell. It was not always so in the Western world. Greco-Roman antiquity had its *daimones*, which is the same word that Christians later used for their demons, but these beings were in fact thought to be quite different kinds of spirits. Daimons existed mid-way between humanity and the gods, and, just like human beings and the Greco-Roman gods, they could be good, bad, or ambivalent in nature. Magicians could call on them to do evil deeds, but not all magic was inherently evil just because it might involve daimons.

In Jewish traditions, such spirits were more thoroughly wicked and opposed to humanity. The apocryphal Book of Enoch, for example, made them into fallen angels who lusted after human women and, after they had seduced them, taught them spells and incantations, herb-lore, astrology, and other magic arts.[51] But canonical Jewish scripture has relatively little to say about demons or the devil. The famous "adversary" (Hebrew: *satan*) of the Book of Job, for example, is by no means the monstrously evil Satan of Christian belief. And in any event, Jewish thought on these matters never became dominant across all ancient Western society as Christianity would in the last few centuries of the Roman Empire. The thorough "demonization of magic," as it has been labeled by the historian Valerie Flint, only occurred in late antiquity, when Christian authorities argued that all pagan daimons were, in fact, Christian demons. As the enormously influential Saint Augustine of Hippo would argue at the end of the fourth century CE, all magical and superstitious arts were "constituted through a certain pestiferous association of human beings and demons, as if by a pact."[52]

Sweeping declarations like this left little room for supposedly natural kinds of magic, but people still tried. Astrology, for example, had an impressive intellectual pedigree stretching back into antiquity, and throughout the Middle Ages some major Christian thinkers continued to regard it as a respectable science that allowed predictions to be made based on the different natural effects astral energies would produce as the stars and other heavenly bodies moved in their course around the fixed Earth. Practitioners of astral magic might also try to attract and focus that energy, still by putatively natural means. For example, gold was thought to have an inherent affinity with the energy of the sun, so a gold medallion could serve to draw that beneficial force to a particular person. Suspicious authorities, however, would look for ways that demons might become involved in the operation, especially if words or symbols were engraved on the medallion, which might serve to communicate with evil spirits.

Alchemists also argued that theirs was an entirely natural art, and alchemical operations were, of course, the root from which modern chemistry eventually grew. But in the Middle Ages, authorities worried that alchemists' long and often highly ritualized processes brought about unnatural transformations that actually depended on the cooperation of demons. Similar suspicions clung to far less elaborate kinds of practice as well. As we've seen, people in medieval Europe might use sage leaves to relieve a fever. So long as this cure was thought to rely only on the inherent properties of the plant, it would be entirely natural. But when people wrote the opening words of the Lord's Prayer on these leaves and fed them to a sick person in a ritualized way over the course of three mornings, the boundaries between the natural and the supernatural began to blur. Authorities became concerned, and condemnations soon flowed.

Still, at no point in European history did people abandon such practices. Neither would they give up on the possibility of positive spiritual magic. Magicians might claim that their practices drew on divine power, calling on saints or angels rather than demons. In the strict bifurcation made by Christian theology, such acts would therefore not be magic at all, but rather prayers, blessings, or devotional rites. To all outward appearances, however, they would be practically the same. Or Christian magicians might admit that they used explicitly demonic invocations, but they could claim to be able to command these evil beings, forcing them into good service. Had not Christ himself promised several times in the Gospels that his followers would gain power over demons in his name?[53] What was exorcism, after all, but a demonic invocation in reverse?

Medieval Christians could even argue that their rites drew on something more like the ambivalent spirits of antiquity. Muslim learning was held in high regard in many intellectual circles in medieval Europe, even as the religion itself was denigrated, and Muslim magical texts carried a good deal of clout. Islam has its devil and its demons, but they are slightly different from their Christian counterparts. In Islamic belief, God created powerful spirits known as jinn separate from the ranks of angels, and unlike angels, jinn have free will. When God then created the first human, Adam, the jinn Iblis refused to bow down to him as God commanded, and so led a portion of his kind into rebellion against the creator and into eternal hostility against humankind. In some schools of Muslim thought, all jinn are evil, but in others, some of them remain ambivalent or even beneficial and protective spirits. The parameters of spiritual magic are therefore more complicated in Islam than in Christianity, even at a purely theoretical level, and actual practice is always murkier still.[54]

Within Christian intellectual systems, Neoplatonism also allowed more space for ambivalent or benevolent spirits than did other modes of thought. For Plato himself, daimons had been important intermediaries between humanity and the divine. Throughout the Middle Ages, and especially after a major Neoplatonic revival in Europe in the Renaissance, this philosophical system allowed some elite magicians, at least, to argue that they practiced an entirely respectable spiritual magic. Not that the majority of Christian authorities were ever terribly receptive to this claim.

Different societies draw the lines between the natural and spiritual worlds in different ways, and they may make those boundaries permeable to some degree. They will also set different moral judgments on various kinds of engagement with the spirit-world, but typically they fix spirits into some moral scheme, while many societies do not attribute any inherent morality to what they believe are entirely natural and non-animate forces or properties. The Western world, and predominantly Christian Europe, provides only one example of how these distinctions intertwine and conflict with one another. What is true around the world, however, is that what each society perceives as magic often exists at the indistinct and contested junctures between these divisions. At the end of this chapter, therefore, as in the previous one, we see that the essence of magic is its imprecise and undetermined nature. No matter how neatly we try to categorize various kinds of magical practices, we will always find that reality is more of a jumble than our categories can encompass.

## NOTES

1 In 1662, Hans Tiehman, a roofer in Brunswick, Germany, consulted Anna Roleffes about various stolen goods, including some sausages; he later accused her of witchcraft: *The Trial of Tempel Anneke: Records of a Witchcraft Trial in Brunswick, Germany, 1663*, ed. Peter A. Morton, trans. Barbara Dähms (Toronto, ON: University of Toronto Press, 2006), 7.

2 Frederick H. Cryer, "Magic in Ancient Syria-Palestine and in the Old Testament," in *Witchcraft and Magic in Europe: Biblical and Pagan Societies*, ed. Bengt Ankarloo and Stuart Clark (Philadelphia: University of Pennsylvania Press, 2001), 118.

3 Augustine, *De doctrina Christiana* 2.20(30), ed. Joseph Martin, Corpus Christianorum Series Latina 32 (Turnhout: Brepols, 1962).

4 Robert E. Lerner, "The Pope and the Doctor," *Yale Review* 78, no. 1 (1988/89): 62–79.

5 Jean Gerson, *De erroribus circa artem magicam* and *Contra superstitionum sculpturae leonis*, in *Oeuvres complètes*, ed. Palémon Glorieux, 10 vols. (Paris: Desclée, 1960–1973), 10: 77–90, 131–34.

6 Adam Ashforth, *Witchcraft, Violence, and Democracy in South Africa* (Chicago, IL: University of Chicago Press, 2005), 148–50.

7 Cryer, "Magic in Ancient Syria-Palestine," 44.

8 John G. Gager, *Curse Tablets and Binding Spells from the Ancient World* (Oxford: Oxford University Press, 1992).

9 Xiaohuan Zhao, "Political Uses of Wugu Sorcery in Imperial China: A Cross-Cultural Perspective," *Magic, Ritual, and Witchcraft* 8 (2013): 132–61.

10 Steve A. Smith, "Talking Toads and Chinless Ghosts: The Politics of 'Superstitious' Rumors in the People's Republic of China, 1961–1965," *American Historical Review* 111 (2006): 405–27, at 415.

11 Reference to invulnerability is first found in the Roman poet Statius's first-century CE epic *Achilleid*.

12 Paul Stoller and Cheryl Olkes, *In Sorcery's Shadow: A Memoir of Apprenticeship among the Songhay of Niger* (Chicago, IL: University of Chicago Press, 1987), 175.

13 Catherine Chène, *Juger les vers: Exorcismes et procès d'animaux dans le diocese de Lausanne (XVe-XVIe s.)* (Lausanne: Université de Lausanne, 1995).

14 Smith, "Talking Toads," 411.

15 1 Samuel 28. The "witch" is never labeled as such in any version of the text itself: in the New Revised Standard Version of the Bible, she is a "medium"; in the King James Version, she is a "woman that hath a familiar spirit"; and in the Jewish Publication Society translation of *Tanakh*, she is a "woman who consults ghosts."

16 Smith, "Talking Toads."

17 Peter Geschiere, *The Modernity of Witchcraft: Politics and the Occult in Postcolonial Africa*, trans. Peter Geschiere and Janet Roitman (Charlottesville: University of Virginia Press, 1997), 179.

18 Gager, *Curse Tablets*, 156.

19 Jacob Grimm, *Teutonic Mythology*, trans. James Stevens Stalleybrass, 4 vols. (London: George Bell and Sons, 1882–88), 2: 704.

20 Geschiere, *Modernity of Witchcraft*, 147–48.

21 Basile Ndjio, "*Mokoagne moni*: Sorcery and New Forms of Wealth in Cameroon," in *The Religion of Fools: Superstition Past and Present*, ed. Steve A. Smith and Alan Knight (Oxford: Oxford University Press, 2008), 271–89.

22 Heinrich Kramer, *Malleus Maleficarum* 2.1.7, ed. and trans. Christopher S. Mackay, 2 vols. (Cambridge: Cambridge University Press, 2006); see also *Malleus* 1.9.

23 Richard Kieckhefer, *Magic in the Middle Ages* (Cambridge: Cambridge University Press, 1989), 91.

24 Kramer, *Malleus* 2.2, 1:495–6.

25 Paul Boyer and Stephen Nissenbaum, *Salem Possessed: The Social Origins of Witchcraft* (Cambridge, MA: Harvard University Press, 1974), 1.

26 William of Auvergne, *De legibus* 27, in his *Opera omnia* (Venice, 1591), 90.

27 Michael D. Bailey, *Fearful Spirits, Reasoned Follies: The Boundaries of Superstition in Late Medieval Europe* (Ithaca, NY: Cornell University Press, 2013), 173.

28 Bailey, *Fearful Spirits*, 172.

29 Judith Devlin, *The Superstitious Mind: French Peasants and the Supernatural in the Nineteenth Century* (New Haven, CT: Yale University Press, 1987), 47–48.

30 Bailey, *Fearful Spirits*, 148–49.

31 Barend J. ter Haar, *Telling Stories: Witchcraft and Scapegoating in Chinese History* (Leiden: Brill, 2006), 248, 252–53.

32 Bailey, *Fearful Spirits*, 217–18.

33 Alan Charles Kors and Edward Peters, eds., *Witchcraft in Europe, 400–1700: A Documentary History*, 2nd ed. (Philadelphia: University of Pennsylvania Press, 2001), 129.

34 Eliphas Lévi, *Transcendental Magic*, trans. Arthur Edward Waite (Boston, MA: Weiser Books, 2001), 238–39.

35 Owen Davies, *Grimoires: A History of Magical Books* (Oxford: Oxford University Press, 2009), 166.

36 Geschiere, *Modernity of Witchcraft*, 50.

37 Margaret J. Wiener, *Visible and Invisible Realms: Power, Magic, and Colonial Conquest in Bali* (Chicago, IL: University of Chicago Press, 1995), 59–60.

38 Yvonne P. Chireau, *Black Magic: Religion and the African American Conjuring Tradition* (Berkeley: University of California Press, 2003), 23.

39 Lucan, *Pharsalia* 6, lines 521–22.

40 Edward Evan Evans-Pritchard, *Witchcraft, Oracles, and Magic among the Azande*, abridged ed. (Oxford: Clarendon, 1976), 58–59.

41 Hans Dieter Betz, ed., *The Greek Magical Papyri in Translation: Including the Demotic Spells*, 2nd ed. (Chicago, IL: University of Chicago Press, 1992), xli–xlii.

42 Michael A. Morgan, trans., *Sepher-ha-Razim: The Book of Mysteries* (Atlanta, GA: Society of Biblical Literature, 1983).

43 Lawrence M. Principe, *The Secrets of Alchemy* (Chicago, IL: University of Chicago Press, 2013), 30–31.

44 Wiener, *Visible and Invisible Realms*, 82–84.

45 Chireau, *Black Magic*, 47–48.

46 Kieckhefer, *Magic in the Middle Ages*, 158.

47  Pliny, *Natural History* 25.94.

48  Josephus, *Jewish War* 7.6.3; R. K. Harrison, "The Mandrake and the Ancient World," *The Evangelical Quarterly* 28, no. 2 (1956): 87–92.

49  Ashforth, *Witchcraft, Violence, and Democracy*, 41–42.

50  Richard Kieckhefer, *Forbidden Rites: A Necromancer's Manual of the Fifteenth Century* (University Park: Pennsylvania State University Press, 1998), 82–85.

51  Enoch 7:10, 8:3–8.

52  Augustine, *De doctrina Christiana* 2.23(36).

53  Matthew 10:1, Mark 3:15, Luke 9:1.

54  For an overview, see Emilie Savage-Smith, ed., *Magic and Divination in Early Islam* (Burlington, VT: Ashgate, 2004).

# MAGIC CONTESTED AND CONDEMNED

Magic, as we have already seen in the first two chapters, is deeply contested terrain. What often defines magic, in fact, is its contested nature, as opposed to the frequently related but putatively more stable and socially accepted domains of religion and science. And of all the contestations surrounding magic, perhaps none are so consequential as debates about two basic issues: whether magic is essentially real or unreal (its practice being either deliberately fraudulent or just unfounded and erroneous), and whether it is good or evil. The first is an intellectual judgment. Depending on how a given society understands the physical world to operate, including how spiritual forces may interact with physical matter, that society may or may not accept that magical practices can produce real and direct effects. The second is obviously a moral determination, imputing positive or negative value to magical acts. The first distinction could be seen as reflecting the judgment of science on magic, while the second very often reflects the judgment of religion.

Of course, these apparent dichotomies are rarely drawn so strictly. Even in societies that by and large attribute real power to magical practices, there will always be some practices that are judged to be false or phony, and hence the domain only of con-men and rubes. In terms of moral censure, even if a society looks upon magical practices disapprovingly, as many have done and continue to do, still a wide gamut of reaction is possible. Practitioners of magic might be vaguely strange and disreputable, or they could be committed agents of evil against whom the full force of legalized torture and judicially sanctioned execution must be brought to bear. Where judicial authorities cannot or will not take such measures (perhaps because they do not believe that magic can produce any real, harmful effects), individuals can take matters into their own hands. In the European city of Ghent, an enraged crowd once eviscerated a suspected sorceress and paraded her stomach around the town. That happened in the year 1128. In Sicily, a man who believed that a woman had killed one of his children through witchcraft broke into her bedroom at night, poured gasoline over her, and set her on fire. That happened in 1904.[1] In parts of Africa and other regions of the non-Western world, where belief in the real power of malevolent magic remains widespread, but where governments still often (although by no means always) eschew witch trials in the name of modernity, mob justice against suspected witches can erupt with dismal regularity.

As these examples show, there can be considerable disagreement within a society as to whether magic is real or not, as well as wicked or not. Western Europe provides a sharp example of both kinds of friction. The essence of Western modernity, at least according to some observers, is its disenchantment. Ever since the eighteenth-century Enlightenment, Western elites have largely denied the reality of magic. Courts will not accept accusations of magical crimes, and if they prosecute magicians, diviners, or witches of any sort, it is usually for fraud, not for acts of magic per se. Nevertheless, countless people in modern Western societies continue to put at least some credence in certain forms of magic. Whether earnestly or lightheartedly, they consult astrologers, attend séances, turn to traditional remedies rather than professional physicians and scientific medicine when they are ill, hang up horseshoes or carry rabbits' feet to attract good luck, or throw salt over their shoulders to ward off evil. Conversely, before the Enlightenment, when Europe's judicial, intellectual, and religious leaders (who were often one and the same) agreed that magic posed a real, demonically inspired threat to Christian society, many people continued to turn to spells, charms, amulets, and rites for peering into the future without much apparent worry about the supposed connection between these practices and diabolical evil.

Despite such spectrums of response, how either the majority of people in a society view magic, or just how a powerful elite may view it, in both intellectual and moral terms, profoundly shapes how magic exists within that society and how suspected or self-declared practitioners of magic will be treated. The most severe repercussions are ultimately legal ones, since these can be backed up by the full weight of political and judicial power. In this chapter, I will treat intellectual, moral, and legal responses in turn, drawing examples from across the globe and throughout history. I will conclude, though, with a focused discussion of the major witch hunts of late medieval and early modern Europe. These constitute by far the most well-studied example of the vigorous condemnation magic has sometimes suffered, and they allow us to see how all the major areas of debate and contestation can interact to sometimes dire effect across an entire society.

## INTELLECTUAL CONTESTATIONS

Incredulity toward magic is often thought to be a paradigmatically modern attitude. In Chapter 1, we saw how some late-nineteenth- and early-twentieth-century anthropologists considered belief in magic to be a trait common to "primitive cultures." This was, in fact, the title of the book in which Edward Tylor, the "father of Anthropology" in Britain, argued that human societies naturally evolved away from reliance on magical beliefs and practices as they became more sophisticated. A few decades later, James Frazer posited in *The Golden Bough* that human societies moved progressively, although not necessarily smoothly, from belief in magic to more advanced forms of religion and finally to scientific rationality. In fact, however, history shows that most societies have been, and continue to be, skeptical about some aspects of what might be labeled as magic, even while they may attribute real and sometimes terrifying power to others. As we also saw in Chapter 1, many societies have considered beliefs and practices from foreign cultures to be magical, and for all that the mysterious "other" can inspire fear, people also tend to be confident that their own cultural beliefs are true while those of strange foreigners must be false or deluded. Then within any given society, people who represent an intellectual or cultural elite are often eager to deride what they present as the foolish magical beliefs of ordinary folk.

The Greek historian Herodotus supplies an elegant example of the sort of intellectual derision that can undercut the fearful power of foreign magicians at a stroke, to which I already alluded in my

Introduction. In Book 7 of his *Histories*, he recounts the Persian emperor Xerxes's invasion of mainland Greece. As Xerxes's huge fleet worked its way down the Aegean coast, it was struck by a terrible storm that raged for three days. According to even the most conservative reports, over four hundred ships were smashed. Finally, the Persian priests, the *magoi*, were moved to action, offering sacrifices and singing incantations to quiet the winds. Their power caused the storm to subside on the fourth day, or, as Herodotus slyly suggests at the end of his long and otherwise credulous account, "perhaps it abated of its own accord."[2]

For a member of an intellectual elite casting aspersions on magical practices common in his own society, one can hardly find a better example than the Roman author Pliny the Elder, whom we have also met already in Chapter 1. His compendious *Natural History* is full of accounts of magical and medicinal rites, with wondrous powers attributed to minerals, plants, animal parts, and even human effluvia. Pliny maintains a resolutely sardonic attitude toward most of them, although he is completely accepting of some. Of healing incantations in general, for example, he notes that "all our wisest men reject belief in them, although as a body the public at all times believes in them unconsciously." Omens, he thinks, have no power to shape the future other than what we give them, by fearfully altering our own behavior. He admits that certain spells used against hail, burns, or diseases have been "tested by experience" and found to be effective, but he is still "very shy of quoting them" because learned opinion about them varies considerably.[3]

Pliny is confident that the practice of placing a whetstone used to sharpen blades under the pillow of a poisoned man in order to cause him to name whoever poisoned him is one of the "lies of the Magi" that have been imported into Roman society.[4] Overall, he considers the Magi to be "the most empty sort of people" (*generis vanissimi*), implying that they are liars and frauds. Apparently, however, their power is sometimes real and needs to be warded off. To protect an entire household from their magical arts, he recommends that women's menstrual blood be smeared on the doorposts of the house. "There is nothing," Pliny asserts, "that I would more willingly believe." In fact, Pliny believes that menstrual blood possesses a number of wondrous properties. If a menstruating woman walks through a cornfield, for example, she will drive away all cat-erpillars, worms, and other vermin. Some say that menstrual blood can also quell lightning and hail, but Pliny thinks that claims like that are "wild indeed."[5]

It is easy to poke fun at Pliny when he violates our modern sense of scientific rationality, just as it is easy to applaud him when his skepticism conforms to ours. The point, though, is not that he was at some points presciently modern and at others hopelessly primitive. At all times he was making what he considered to be reasoned and serious distinctions, although his bases for drawing those distinctions differ from those that would be employed by any modern scientist. Scores of other ancient authors reasoned likewise, rejecting foreign rites and also common practices in their own cul-ture that they thought were foolish and ineffective, while still fully accepting many other practices that they regarded as wondrous, mysterious, and perhaps even explicitly magical.

Early Christian authors who would set much of the tone for subsequent Western European ideas of magic followed their Roman forebears very closely in some ways. Augustine of Hippo, later to be Saint Augustine, who lived several centuries after Pliny, quoted a joke that he attributed to the even earlier Roman writer Cato in order to show his scorn for people who took certain omens seri-ously. Finding that one's clothing had been infested by mice was often taken as an omen of even greater impending suffering, and a man who discovered that his boots had been gnawed by mice once reported this to Cato. The sober statesman supposedly replied that there was nothing to worry about, although it would have been an "ill omen indeed if the mice had been gnawed on by the boots."[6] In other respects, though, Augustine took matters of magic very seriously indeed, attributing most magical practices to demons and warning Christians of their dangerous power. Yet medieval Christian writers did not always take the power of demons so seri-ously. In the early tenth century, the legal text known as the canon *Episcopi* (from its first word in Latin: "bishops") described groups of women traveling through the night in the train of a demon, who they thought was the pagan goddess, Diana. This later became a standard reference point for the idea of witches flying at night to a sabbath in Western European thought. But the canon itself declares this nocturnal journey to be nothing but an illusion: "who is so stupid and foolish," it proclaims, "as to think that all these things which are done in spirit happen in the body."[7]

While most intellectual authorities in medieval Europe accepted the real power of demons, magic, and the supernatural, even in that period some intellectuals could exhibit a much greater degree of skepticism. One such thinker was Nicole Oresme, who lived in France in the fourteenth century. In a book *On the Causes of Wonders*, he argued that most apparent wonders were neither demonic magic nor divine miracle. When trying to explain them, he cautioned that "there is no need to turn immediately to the heavens, the last refuge of the pitiful, or to demons, or to glorious God." If one looked closely, some kind of natural causation could almost always be discerned.[8] Other medieval traditions had similar skeptics. The Muslim jurist Abu Bakr al-Jassas, who lived in Baghdad in the tenth century, argued that most magic was nothing but deceit and trickery. Like some European thinkers, he mocked the idea that spells could transform people into animals, or that people could fly through the air on brooms (or jars or ostrich eggs). The sort of people who most typically believed in magic, he contended, were "the ignorant masses and the women among us," a phrase that also echoes much medieval European invective.[9] Likewise in Judaism, the twelfth-century philosopher Moses Maimonides argued in his famous *Guide to the Perplexed* that most magic was complete nonsense.[10]

Of course, such voices were relatively rare in the Western world during the Middle Ages. By and large, magic was accepted as real and efficacious in Christian, Jewish, and Muslim intellectual traditions. Yet none of these traditions accepted the absolute reality of all forms of magical practice. The extreme skeptics that I have listed above are often described as proto-modern and ahead of their times. They were, however, nothing of the kind. They simply pushed entirely medieval forms of skepticism about the reality of magic further than did most other thinkers.

A more robust skepticism about magical practices having any real effect on the physical world took broader hold, at least among intellectual elites, in the seventeenth and eighteenth centuries. This was the era of the Scientific Revolution and Enlightenment in Europe, and the rise of modern science has often been credited with freeing Western societies from their "medieval" magical superstitions. In fact, many early scientific thinkers continued to accept the reality of certain systems of magic and in some cases to draw inspiration from them. In the mid-sixteenth century, for example, the astronomer Nicholas Copernicus did not formulate his heliocentric theory because of new empirical observations or discoveries. He was instead inspired to hypothesize that the sun rather than the earth stood at the center of the universe in part because of the important role that the sun played in magical Hermetic philosophy that was then very much in vogue.[11] Subsequently, a number of major figures associated with the Scientific Revolution continued to believe in magic and witchcraft, or to practice astrology or alchemy.

An important development of the Scientific Revolution that could be profoundly anti-magical was the advance of so-called mechanical philosophy. It held that the universe operated like a giant mechanism, driven only by direct physical interactions between matter with no possibility of occult or spiritual forces such as might operate in magic. The French philosopher René Descartes, famous for postulating the separation of mind and body, was an adherent to this school of thought. The most famous figure of the Scientific Revolution, however, was not. The invisible, immaterial force of gravity that Isaac Newton determined was central to universal motion was derided by many strict mechanical philosophers as magical. As I noted briefly in Chapter 1, the German philosopher and mathematician Gottfried Wilhelm Leibniz called it both "a supernatural thing" and "an occult impulse" that must be either "miraculous or imaginary."[12]

The success of Newton's gravitational theory notwithstanding, major thinkers of the European Enlightenment drew on mechanical philosophy to argue that neither magic nor miracles played any real role in the physical universe. In the early 1690s, the Dutch pastor Balthasar Bekker's fully skeptical *De Betoverde Weereld* (The World Bewitched) drew in part on the Cartesian separation of spirit and matter to argue that demons exerted no real power in the physical world, and hence no real effects could be attributed to forms of magic that claimed to draw on such spiritual entities. Already in 1670, Bekker's countryman Baruch Spinoza had argued that miracles were not real, as did the English philosopher David Hume in the mid-1700s.

The seemingly inherent relationship between demonic and divine power caused many Christian thinkers at this time to voice great concerns that any complete denial of the reality of magic would also lead to denial of the real power and perhaps even the existence of God. But as the French *philosophe* Denis Diderot wrote in his *Philosophical Thoughts* in 1746, "superstition is more injurious to God than atheism."[13] This is what magic subsequently became, at least for European intellectual and political elites: a false and powerless superstition. By the early twentieth century, the German sociologist Max Weber would argue that "disenchantment," or the removal of magic from the world, was an essential component of modern European culture.

Of course, the modern world has never been completely disenchanted. Innumerable people continue to believe in some forms of magic, either absolutely or with a certain degree of equivocation, even while they might deny the reality of other kinds of magic completely. This situation is not fundamentally so different from what has been the case in many past societies as well. What differs is a matter of degree. The accepted norms of mainstream modern Western culture deny reality to magic far more extensively than has been the case in any other known human society, past or present. This powerful denial, even if never resolutely accepted, has profoundly affected the practice of magic both in the West and around the world (which we'll investigate more fully in Chapter 6).

Most evidence suggests that cultures around the globe, at least prior to their contact with Europeans, have exhibited characteristics like those described for premodern Western societies above. That is, most societies have accepted the reality of some magical practices while denying others, and within any society, different groups have exhibited different levels of skepticism, with intellectual elites often deriding many magical practices of more ordinary people. As we saw in Chapter 2, for example, the seventeenth-century Chinese author Wang Bu mocked many common protective spells, although he quickly used the so-called "Spell of Tianpeng" himself when he thought that he had encountered a demon. Of course, we almost always have better records and sources regarding the attitudes of elites, no matter where or when they have lived, than we do for the beliefs and practices of ordinary people. Moreover, for many societies the evidence we have of their magical beliefs altogether prior to the arrival of Europeans is scant, and contact with Europe has often brought great changes to magical systems.

As European states began to expand into colonial empires in the sixteenth and seventeenth centuries, they were not shy about imposing their ideas about magic onto other societies and judging them accordingly. Indigenous beliefs and practices that might have been justifiably labeled religious or scientific, that is, socially sanctioned, respectable, and operating according to understood and agreed-upon principles within a given society, were instead labeled magic because they did not conform to European ideas of religion and science. The patronizing attitude that European rulers often had as they spread their authority around the globe was not without some positive consequences. When the Spanish Inquisition arrived in the Americas in the sixteenth century, for example, it did not prosecute natives for witchcraft or other magical crimes, because it judged them to be too simple and not yet sufficiently educated in true religion to understand what they were doing. The correction of what Europeans perceived as demonically infused native practices was left to (often no less brutal) missionaries or secular authorities.

Later, during the nineteenth-century heyday of European imperialism around the globe, colonial administrators saw it as their duty to combat native primitivism and to impose a more modern, disenchanted sensibility that involved denying any reality to native magical practices. In many regions, this meant eliminating traditional means by which people had protected themselves from perceived harmful magic or witchcraft. Such protection often involved counter-magic of various kinds, but it could also involve using divination to identify magicians and witches, and then threatening or even killing those people to break their spells. Subsequently, in some areas of Africa and elsewhere in the post-colonial world, legal witch hunting has been revived as part of an effort to reassert traditional cultures and repudiate imposed European norms. In other places, the lynching of suspected witches has become increasingly common, as legal authorities still refuse to recognize and prosecute witchcraft as a real crime, but society believes in its harmful power and is ready to sanction even extreme and violent means of redress and protection.[14]

## MORAL DEBATES

Even in societies that for the most part deny any effective reality to magic, magicians can still be seen as morally suspect people, and they can be accused of fraud for claiming to have special powers. Likewise, people who continue to believe in the reality of magic after some powerful segment of their society has declared it to be unreal can be tarred as ignorant fools who cause real social harm by perpetuating superstitious modes of thinking. In fact, since no society ever believes universally in all aspects of magic, these forms of moral censure can always be present, and I'll discuss a few examples that fall into this category. Mainly, however, I want to focus here on the more serious and potentially damning kinds of moral debates that emerge when a society largely accepts that magic can have real power and that magicians are therefore capable of both astoundingly beneficial and terribly harmful acts. The basic possibilities, in terms of moral judgment, would be that magic is entirely good, that it is inherently ambiguous, or that it is utterly evil, and I will explore each in turn.

In practice, we can dismiss the first possibility. No society has ever judged magic to be wholly good. By the very nature of how magic is typically defined, if practices are not at least a little mysterious, uncertain, risky, or risqué, then they tend to get shifted into the more socially respectable categories of religion or science. This is not to say that religions are not often mysterious or that science is not full of uncertainty, but such matters are usually framed within systems that are perceived to be stable and socially acceptable. Practices understood as magical, by contrast, tend to exist more on the fringes of a society rather than at its well-regulated center. This does not mean that such practices need be rare. They are often ubiquitous within a society, but they lack a certain level of official sanction: a healing rite performed by a local woman with a reputation for wielding extraordinary power rather than by a designated physician, for example, or an incantation pronounced by such a woman instead of by a designated priest. This also does not mean that individual practitioners of magic cannot or do not perceive their own actions as being entirely good. They will, however, be viewed with some level of suspicion by other members of their society.

Neo-pagan Witchcraft offers a particularly rich example of this dynamic, even though it exists within the modern Western world that largely denies the reality of magic. Modern Witches consider their practices to be a religion (although some eschew that weighted word in favor of terms like "spiritual path" instead). Yet they also explicitly label a set of their practices as magic, which they believe has real power. Against utterly bogus charges of Satanism or demon-worship that are sometimes lodged against them, they are quick to assert the strongly positive nature of the magical forces they claim to wield, but there is no doubt that their society places them somewhat on its fringe. Moreover, despite the rapid growth in numbers of self-proclaimed Witches in many Western societies in the late twentieth and early twenty-first centuries, they often still see themselves as deliberate outsiders within a larger culture whose mainstream values they at least partially reject.

Yet even if neo-pagan Witchcraft were to become numerically mainstream, it might remain discernibly "magical" since many of its practitioners stress the dramatic fluidity of their practices. Among some modern Witches, some rites have become fairly set and formalized, but for many, the essence of their practice is the innovation of new rites, either individually or in small, independent groups. Thus, Witchcraft tends to lack the sort of institutional structures and stable rituals that contribute to the social respectability of many other established religions. Perhaps closest to neo-pagan Witchcraft in this regard in the modern world are the fluid Afro-American religions of the Caribbean and Latin America, such as Candomblé, Santería, and Vodou. And these religions, too, are often regarded as more "magical" by outsiders, and even by their own practitioners, than are other common Western religious systems.

For all its fluidity, modern Witchcraft is not devoid of what might be called doctrine. A basic moral principle accepted by many Witches is expressed in the Wiccan rede: "An it harm none, do what ye will." Another controlling mechanism is the so-called law of three. Most, although by no means all, Witches and other kinds of neo-pagan magical practitioners assert that whatever is done through magic will rebound on the practitioner three-fold.[15] Hence it is wise to practice only good and not harmful magic. But self-evidently these statements also express the belief that magic can be used to harm or for other nefarious ends. This built-in ambiguity is frequently seized upon in film and television, which often delight in presenting powerful Witches "gone bad" and using their magic for great evil, until they get their moral come-uppance.[16]

So we return once again to the normal and perhaps the defining status of magic being ambiguity. Deserved or not, a cloud of moral ambiguity hangs over many who claim to practice magic or who are perceived to practice it. This is true around the world in the modern period. In Africa, traditional healers often serve to identify and combat witches. Nevertheless, even those who patronize them also sometimes fear them as a potential source of harm, for their power is often thought to be essentially the same as that of a maleficent witch.[17] Likewise, many practitioners of Caribbean or South American systems such as of Candomblé or Santería may believe that the powers they invoke can be either helpful or harmful.[18] Beyond such internal ambiguities, external voices often seek to define these systems as entirely harmful, corrupt, and wicked. Pentecostal preachers inveigh against Candomblé as a form of devil-worship in South America, for example, as both Christian and Muslim preachers do against traditional practices in Africa.[19]

Similar patterns are evident throughout history. Trying to understand magical practices in the depths of antiquity, scholars often struggle to grasp the various meanings of certain basic terms, which could fluctuate over time (as we saw in Chapter 1). The Greek *goeteia* originally meant a ritual lament over the dead, but it came to apply to a range of darkly chthonic rites for summoning spirits. *Pharmakeia* described the use, potentially quite beneficial, of any kind of medicine or drug, but it also carried overtones of harmful potions and poisons. In Latin, *veneficium* carried even clearer harmful implications (leading to the English "venomous"), but it could still sometimes be used in a fairly neutral sense.

Of all ancient Western societies, that of the Hebrews can appear to be the most thoroughly negative toward magic. Numerous biblical injunctions seem to condemn almost all magic. The most famous, of course, is Exodus 22:18, "you shall not permit a sorceress to live," but there are others, such as the far more detailed statement in Deuteronomy 18:10–12:

> No one shall be found among you [...] who practices divination, or is a soothsayer, or an augur, or a sorcerer, or one who casts

spells, or who consults ghosts of spirits, or who seeks oracles from the dead. For whoever does these things is abhorrent to the Lord.

Nevertheless, Hebrew priests regularly performed an oracular practice involving objects known as *Urim* and *Thummim* (e.g. Numbers 27:21, 1 Samuel 14:41), which they appear to have used to make yes-or-no designations and predictions, akin to casting lots.

Perhaps most ambiguously of all, the most famous practitioner of putatively illicit divination mentioned in the Bible, the woman who only much later came to be known as the "witch" of Endor, appears in the original text as an entirely helpful figure. As we've seen, the Hebrew king Saul secretly consults with her before a major battle, after other forms of priestly divination, including *Urim* and *Thummim*, have failed him. She summons the spirit of the dead prophet Samuel, who tells Saul in no uncertain terms that he is going to lose both the battle and his life. The king is visible shaken and collapses upon hearing this news, at which point the hospitable medium insists that he eat some of her food to regain his strength before going on his way (1 Samuel 28:3–25).

If anything, Judaism became more tolerant of magic as it aged. Rabbinic interpretations of scripture from the first through fifth centuries CE explicitly sanctioned rites intended to heal injuries or to protect from other harmful forms of magic. Rabbis could themselves be practitioners of magic, and the Babylonian Talmud tells of two hungry rabbis who once conjured up a calf for their evening meal.[20] Early Islam likewise recognized both good and bad kinds of magic. The twelfth-century scholar Fakhr al-Din al-Razi (d. 1209) argued in his commentary on the Qur'an that there was nothing wrong with wise men studying various kinds of occult rites. Their goal should be to distinguish licit from illicit practice, because magic was not evil in itself, although it could, of course, be used for evil ends.[21]

Magic used to perform harmful acts can readily be declared to be wicked. Likewise, magic can be made to seem morally questionable if it is strongly associated with people who are judged to be in some way morally suspicious, be they foreigners, the lower classes, or women (depending on one's own condemning stance). But such assertions can also be readily challenged. Practitioners can point to the good that they do, or claim to do, and maintain that they are not the bad sort of people who perform the bad sort of magic. A more inflexible kind of moral condemnation is to argue that magic always draws on inherently evil powers, no matter who uses it or to what end. Among the most thorough attempts at this kind of moral condemnation in world history came from Christian authorities, beginning in the early days of the church, extending through the medieval and early modern periods, and in many ways continuing into the modern era as well. As Christianity gained ascendency in the late Roman Empire (the third through fifth centuries), church leaders asserted that all magical practices depended on demons, as did pagan religious practices, which they now reclassified as magic. And since demons were inherently evil, so was all magic, no matter who might perform it, under what circumstances, or toward what ends.

To some extent, this sharp bifurcation resulted from Christianity's sharply divided moral universe, split between God and the devil. In fact, however, the extent of Christianity's "demonization of magic" was far greater than anything ever propounded by the two other major Western monotheisms. Judaism was never as obsessed with its fallen angels as Christianity became, and we've seen that Islam maintained that jinn, while often wicked, were not necessarily always evil. From antiquity into the medieval period, neither religion maintained as stark a stance against magic as did Christianity. But even within Christianity, there was ambiguity. Especially in the later medieval and early modern periods, Christian thinkers developed categories of natural magic, which claimed to draw only on occult forces in nature rather than on spiritual ones, and they also presented certain forms of explicitly spiritual magic as theurgy, that is, as drawing on divine or angelic power rather than demonic. Such arguments never won widespread support from church authorities, but they were still developed within a thoroughly Christian framework.

Meanwhile, as arcane debated raged among the intelligentsia, ordinary people seem always to have focused more on the results that magic could supposedly be used to obtain than on its inherent nature, although they were of course also deeply affected by their church's message that magic was inherently demonic and evil. We'll see some of the more gruesome effects of that message in the final section of this chapter, on witch hunts in Western Europe.

Those horrors notwithstanding, the conclusion here must be that even within what might be characterized as the profoundly anti-magical culture of the Christian West, magic was always the subject of moral debate, as it has been and continues to be around the world.

## LEGAL CONDEMNATIONS

Moral censure obviously informs the legal condemnations that the use of magic has faced in many societies. Some surprising disjunctures can also exist, however, between general moral castigation and the criminalization of specific magical acts. Here we will see yet again how no society has ever had completely stable and fixed ideas of what magic might be or what it could do, and how different groups within the same society can hold quite disparate and even conflicting ideas. In the legal sphere, this often leads to skeptical authorities refusing to prosecute magical crimes as assiduously as people want, while in other cases more credulous and aggressive authorities might try to provoke people to make accusations and bring cases to court when they are not inclined to do so. In legal adjudications, as in moral debates, authorities may choose to focus on the results that magic is thought to achieve, and in such cases, they will condemn magic when it is used to kill, to steal, or to commit other criminal acts. The other possibility is to condemn and criminalize magic per se, regardless of how it is used. Efforts toward this more complete kind of criminalization can appear in highly credulous and fearful societies, such as Europe during the period of its major witch hunts, but they can also appear in highly skeptical societies. When legal authorities lose any belief in the reality of magic to cause specific outcomes, they may then criminalize all magical practices, regardless of their intended effects, as fraud.

The tension between condemning specific magical practices used to achieve harmful effects or condemning all magic per se, because it is believed to be morally or spiritually corrupting, is evident throughout history. The Code of Hammurabi, composed in Mesopotamia in the eighteenth century BCE, mentions the possibility of bringing a legal accusation against someone suspected of performing spells against another person. The term used (*kispu*) implies a harmful rite, and the code prescribes death for the accused if the charge is proven (or death for the accuser if it is not). We've already encountered the famous biblical injunction in Exodus 22:18, "you shall not permit a sorceress to live." Again, the word used (*mekhashefah*) implies a woman practicing some form of harmful magic. Leviticus 20:27 is slightly broader, ordering that "a man or woman who is a medium or a wizard" should be stoned to death. As we've also seen, however, Hebrew society was not so strict in practice. When King Saul cracked down on practitioners of magic in his realm, he "expelled the mediums and wizards from the land" (1 Samuel 28:3), but he did not execute them. When later he needed to consult a diviner himself, before his fatal battle with the Philistines, his servants knew exactly where to find one, in the town of Endor.

Ancient Greece yields little surviving legislation against magical activities, but in records of court cases involving magic, the charges almost always focus on harm caused by magical means, rather than on the use of magic itself. One of the few law codes addressing magic that does survive, from the Ionian city of Teos on what is now the Aegean coast of Turkey, refers specifically to *pharmaka deleteria*, or harmful drugs, which presumes that other forms of *pharmaka* considered beneficial were not criminalized.[22] The Greeks did have a legal charge of "impiety" (*asebia*), for which courts could impose a death sentence, and the Hippocratic text *On the Sacred Disease* implies that practitioners of magic, in general, should be charged with this crime.[23] Overall, however, Greek sources offer little indication that all magicians were automatically considered impious, at least in the legal sense.

In ancient Rome, we can see a clear change over time in how magic was criminalized. The early legal code known as the Twelve Tables legislated against magic (in Table 8), but specified that only *malum carmen* (an evil spell) should be prosecuted. One of the major laws under which magic was prosecuted for much of the Roman period was the *Lex Cornelia de sicariis et veneficiis*, issued in 81 BCE. The context makes clear that only *veneficium* as harmful poisoning was being targeted (*sicarius* means "assassin" or "murderer"). Over time, however, the Romans' concept of *veneficium* expanded, and by 300 CE an important legal commentary on the *Lex Cornelia* argued that it applied to magical practices more broadly.[24] Already by that time, however, another term, *maleficium*, was becoming increasingly common in Roman law. Originally it had meant any kind of "evil deed," but by the third century CE it had become the most common word for harmful, criminalized magic.

Despite some blurring of boundaries due to sweeping terminology, the distinction between beneficial and harmful magic remained fairly well-fixed in Roman law even as the empire Christianized and ultimately crumbled in the West. Most law codes in early medieval Europe also stressed harm done by magical means, not the inherently wicked nature of all magic, even though Christian religious authorities steadily proclaimed that all magic was demonic and evil. In the eastern half of the Roman world, which historians call the Byzantine Empire, law codes continued to tolerate beneficial magic until the ninth century, when the emperor Leo VI issued new edicts that dealt with magic in a more sweeping and severe way.[25] The legal status of magic also changed for the worse in Western Europe, but we'll examine that history more fully in the final section of this chapter.

In imperial China, governments legislated against magic in various ways at least since the Tang dynasty, founded in the seventh century CE, and through the Qing dynasty, which ended in 1912. Under Qing law, magic was partially addressed under the so-called "Ten Abominations." These were not specific statutes but more a statement of basic moral positions that should guide jurists, and they, in fact, reflect principles going back to the Tang period. They deal with magic in terms of poisoning, directing a demonic spirit to attack someone and other clearly harmful acts. More specific statutes also tend to focus on harmful magical acts, as well as on improper forms of divination. Yet other statutes ban the use of magic to "delude" gullible people, thus showing how legislation could extend both to practices that authorities believed could produce real effects and to practices that they judged to be ineffectual but socially harmful nonetheless.[26] In modern Communist China, the government regards all magical practices as false, unreal, and a harmful vestige of "feudal superstition," but it has also set its security services to monitor reports of such beliefs and practices as a way to chart popular attitudes deemed to be potentially dangerous to the state.[27]

In parts of the world that have experienced European colonization, the legal status of magic often reflects the complex interplay of native traditions and imposed European norms. We've already seen how, in Spanish colonies in Central and South America, the Inquisition had legal jurisdiction over practices classified as magic, superstition, and witchcraft, but it did not include native people in its jurisdiction because it deemed that their understanding of Christianity was not yet sufficiently developed to be policed in that way. One of the most interesting legal histories in the New World, however, comes from the former French colony of Haiti.[28] The colonial "Code Noir," first issued in 1685 and intended to regulate slave populations, classified many aspects of African spirituality among slaves in the colony as "sorcery" (*sortilège*). Eventually, rites termed *le vaudoux* became a major legal and political concern, since they entailed gatherings of potentially rebellious Africans. Vodou "dances" did, in fact, play a role in the great slave rebellions that produced the Haitian revolution. As the revolutionary leader, Toussaint Louverture, secured power, however, he too passed ordinances against *le vaudoux* as dangerous to political stability, and when Haitian independence was formally established in 1804, the government immediately began suppressing *danses de vodou* by military force.

By 1835, independent Haiti followed colonial precedent and classified Vodou as "sorcery." By this, the Haitian government intended to signal its acceptance of modern Western legal principles, but it went against most Haitians' traditional understandings, for there exists within the system of Vodou a specific category of harmful magic, *maji*, which Vodou itself is intended to protect against. Nevertheless, ordinary Haitians also turned the law code to their benefit. Sometimes when Vodou rites failed to provide promised benefits or protection, disgruntled clients would turn the Vodou practitioner over to authorities as a sorcerer. After the 1860s, when the Haitian government reclassified Vodou as ineffective superstition rather than harmful sorcery, practitioners could still be prosecuted for committing fraud.

In the second half of the twentieth century, the regimes of "Papa Doc" and "Baby Doc" Duvalier promoted Vodou rites as an aspect of native African culture, but they also kept the regulation against superstition on the books so that they could control the political use of Vodou and the activities of any of its practitioners. The Haitian government only officially decriminalized Vodou in 1987, but authorities continued to perform some extra-judicial arrests, often under public pressure to act against perceived harmful sorcery. This, too, is a dynamic evident elsewhere in the modern postcolonial world. In societies in which large segments of the population still believe in the reality of many forms of magic, but where legal authorities follow the Western model of denying all magic as ineffectual fraud, extra-judicial but socially supported forms of punishment inflicted on suspected witches can be a serious problem. In the mid-1990s, for example, South Africa considered revising its legal code to accept the reality of witchcraft and impose penalties on anyone proven to practice it. Importantly, the revisions would also have punished anyone making unsupported accusations, including using any magical means or employing another magician to identify a witch.[29]

Proving charges made against witches, sorcerers, and other agents of suspected harmful magic often poses problems for legal authorities. Since magic tends to be a mysterious and occult activity, it rarely leaves many witnesses or much clearly incriminating evidence beyond suspicion and rumor. Authorities seeking to oppose magic often find themselves forced to rely on other magical or at least supernatural means to identify and convict an accused magician. As noted above, the ancient Code of Hammurabi addressed the possibility of a legal accusation made against a sorcerer. In fact, however, trials seem to have occurred only rarely, if ever, in ancient Mesopotamia. Instead, people turned to counter-magic to protect themselves. What the Code describes is a way either to prove or disprove an otherwise unsubstantiated charge of harmful magic.

> If a man charge a man with sorcery, and cannot prove it, he who is charged with sorcery shall go to the river, into the river he shall throw himself and if the river overcome him, his accuser shall take to himself his house (estate). If the river show that man to be innocent and he come forth unharmed, he who charged him with sorcery shall be put to death.[30]

In modern societies that still largely accept the reality of harmful magic, people often turn to traditional healers and diviners to identify when an illness or injury has been caused by witchcraft, and perhaps to identify the witch as well. If courts become involved, they must decide how far they will accept such testimony.

Another common means of proving an accusation of a magical crime is through the confession of the accused. Since people do not often confess willingly to crimes that may carry penalties as severe as exile or death, courts throughout history have often found themselves relying on torture and other extreme measures to gather what they hope will be reliable evidence. Western Europe provides one of the best examples of this dismal dynamic, so that is where we will now turn.

## WITCHES AND WITCH HUNTS IN WESTERN EUROPE

As we've seen, throughout the medieval period the Christian church in Western Europe declared magic to be demonic and inherently evil. For centuries, however, secular law codes continued to focus only on those forms of magic perceived to cause direct harm. Even in church law, the canon *Episcopi* only required church authorities to exile practitioners of "sorcery and witchcraft" from their territories. Also, *Episcopi* and other sources stressed that demonic power was mostly illusory, presenting a spiritual but not a real physical threat. Magic became a much more serious issue during the twelfth and thirteenth centuries. Scholars, most of whom were clergymen themselves, began to study magical texts, and some even began to practice complex ritual magic. The concerns of other church authorities were raised.[31]

Europe also underwent a major legal shift, largely complete by the thirteenth century, from accusatorial to inquisitorial procedure. Under accusatorial procedure, individuals who brought accusations to court were responsible for proving them, and if they failed to do so, they would suffer the same punishment as the accused would have if the accusation had been proven. This system reflects a retributive approach to justice that we have seen in operation as far back as the Code of Hammurabi. Because clear evidence of magical crimes was often very hard to come by, this approach appears to have kept a certain lid on wayward accusations. By contrast, under inquisitorial procedure (which would be used not only by church inquisitors but by secular courts as well), once an accusation was made, the court took responsibility for investigating and proving or disproving the charge. Court officials were not penalized in any way for pursuing accusations that turned out to be false. They were simply doing their jobs. This is, of course, the procedure followed in most modern criminal courts, but this modernizing step ironically removed an important safeguard against more rampant accusations of illicit magic.

It was now easier or at least safer for people to accuse their neighbors of being witches, but for courts the problem of proving the charge remained. Not just in cases of magic but with any major crime for which eyewitnesses or physical evidence might be lacking, inquisitorial courts standardly turned to torture to extract a confession from the accused. In medieval Europe, judicial torture was first applied in this way by a secular court in the Italian city of Verona in 1228. Inquisitorial procedure and torture provided the main judicial framework for subsequent witch trials in Western Europe, and this framework was in place by the thirteenth century. Major witch trials, however, did not begin until the fifteenth century. Some ingredient was still missing from the fatal brew.

In the early 1400s, a new and more insidious idea of what witchcraft entailed began to develop in the minds of prosecuting officials. Initially, it was fairly localized to trials taking place in lands surrounding the western Alps, but it would eventually spread across Europe. Authorities increasingly accused witches not just of practicing harmful and inevitably demonic magic, but also of being members of organized diabolical sects that gathered secretly to worship demons, perform abominable acts of murder and wanton sexuality, and plan their attack on Christian society. Initially authorities referred to these gatherings as synagogues, but they soon came to term them witches' sabbaths. From a prosecutorial perspective, the idea of the sabbath added one final element to the framework of witch hunting, namely, that suspected witches could now be pressured into naming other suspects, whom they would have met at these gatherings. Although many other factors were needed to escalate a single trial into a major witch hunt, these three elements – inquisitorial procedure, torture, and the idea that witches conspired in groups – figure in most of the large-scale witch trials that occurred in Europe, beginning in the fifteenth century but centering on the 1500s and 1600s.

Slow in coming, what is sometimes still referred to as the European "witch craze" was also not nearly as extensive or pervasive as it is sometimes presented as being. First, the brutal facts: European courts, including those in European colonies in the New World, executed around 50,000 people as witches from the 1400s until 1782, when the last fully legal execution in Europe took place. In some jurisdictions, the execution rates could rise above 90 percent. That is, if put on trial for witchcraft in those courts, one had less than a one-in-ten chance of surviving. In other jurisdictions, however, execution rates could be 25 percent or below, which was in fact normal for any capital crime in the harsh legal regimes that dominated this period. Moreover, formal accusations and trials were not endemic to Europe. Some regions saw almost no witch trials, ever. In other regions, terrifyingly massive hunts could spiral completely out of control. In the Duchy of Lorrain, for example, sandwiched between France and the German empire, 2,000 executions took place between 1580 and 1620. In the smaller territory around Cologne, courts executed roughly the same number of witches in only a decade, from 1626 to 1635. By contrast, however, across all of England and Scotland courts executed only 1,500 witches in the whole period of the trials. Spain, with an even larger population in these centuries, executed only 300 people as witches.[32]

The terrible ferocity of some witch hunts would prove their undoing. Trials declined and ultimately ended not because European society moved toward complete skepticism about the basic reality of magic or witchcraft, but due to what many scholars have called a more limited sort of "judicial skepticism." Some legal authorities recognized quite early that much of the evidence used in witch trials was simply not reliable: the testimony of other suspected witches, hearsay evidence, sometimes testimony by very young children, and above all confessions extracted through what even early modern society considered to be the excessive use of torture. These factors were often especially important in escalating a contained trial or series of trials into a major hunt. Whenever stricter standards of evidence were enforced, however, and especially whenever torture was banned or even carefully controlled, conviction rates plummeted and accusations dwindled.

No one moment marks the decline of witch trials across all of Europe. Different jurisdictions came to the conclusion that better controls needed to be imposed at different times. The Dutch

Republic held its last legal execution for witchcraft in 1609. The Parlement of Paris, the high court of appeal for most of Northern France, no longer sanctioned any executions for this crime after 1623. In that same year, the Spanish Inquisition instituted new procedural controls, after which its courts executed only a handful of witches. After ending or at least greatly reducing the number of witch trials through stricter judicial controls, many jurisdictions moved on to the full decriminalization of witchcraft. This usually occurred significantly later, however, only after legal and political elites began to reject the basic reality of most forms of magic. In England, for example, witch trials had largely ended by 1650, but the statute declaring witchcraft to be a capital crime was not revoked until 1736. In Spain, witches were still sporadically put on trial as late as 1820.

As I have already noted, however, just because legal authorities may abandon belief in magic, this does not mean that they can no longer prosecute any magicians. Sticking with the English example, under the new legal understanding of witchcraft promulgated in 1736, anyone claiming to be a witch, fortuneteller, traditional healer, or any type of practicing magician could be prosecuted for fraud and might face up to a year in prison. After 1824, such people were more commonly prosecuted under an act against vagrancy. This legal situation persisted until 1951 when both the witchcraft and vagrancy acts were repealed. That, in turn, allowed an ex-civil servant named Gerald Gardener to proclaim himself publically to be a modern Witch and to launch the Wiccan movement with the publication of his book *Witchcraft Today* in 1954. Other countries in Western Europe instituted legal changes at their own pace, but always leading toward the same end. In France, for example, the critical shift came even earlier than in England, when in 1682 Louis XIV redirected legal attention away from putatively real witchcraft and toward "false sorcerers" (*faux sorciers*) who wielded no real power but who deluded both common people and courtly elites alike.

While overall during the Enlightenment European elites moved increasingly toward complete skepticism about magical rites possessing any real, efficacious power, ordinary people appear largely to have clung to their traditional practices. They continued using magical charms for health or protection, and they still feared possible magical assault by others. In many circumstances, they readily turned to semi – or even fully – professional practitioners of magical healing or divination, often called cunning-folk in English, who continued to enjoy a brisk trade as recognized magical experts throughout the nineteenth century and into the twentieth.

This diverse spectrum of engagement with different forms of magic was very much a return to longstanding patterns that had been somewhat disrupted, although never fully displaced, by the surge in legal prosecution of perceived harmful magic during the period of the witch hunts. In fact, European society had believed in witches for centuries before it began to pursue them intensely through legal means, and even as witch trials reached their peak in the late sixteenth and early seventeenth centuries, the most common response to suspected witchcraft or other perceived magical attack was still not to turn immediately to courts and legal prosecution. Remarkably common across many trial records are statements to the effect that individuals had been well known as witches in their communities for years before ever facing formal charges. Rather than rushing to denounce some poor old woman at the first suspicion, as the idea of a pervasive witch-craze might suggest, and as certainly did happen in some large, out-of-control hunts, many people chose to deal with witches they believed to be in their midst through other means, often relying on magic themselves.

The history of magic in Europe is frequently seen as exceptional when placed in a larger global context, both because of the spectacular horrors and elaborate diabolical stereotypes of its major hunts and because of its supposed subsequent disenchantment and rejection of all forms of magic as silly superstition. In fact, however, neither of those historical episodes were quite so absolute. When one looks at other patterns, Europe becomes much more comparable to other regions of the globe. Magic has been and still is frequently condemned, but never completely, and it can be contested and debated from a number of different angles. Even if a society fully accepts the reality of some magical practices, it will be skeptical of others. If it fears the absolute moral corruption of some magical rites, it will nevertheless probably accept the basic usefulness or at least harmlessness of others. Different groups and people at different levels of any given society will always hold ideas about magic that differ to some degree, perhaps quite dramatically. Such differences can become especially notable when legal authorities and courts enforce very different ideas about magic than may be held by much of the populace. These shifting perspectives make magic a very slippery but very important part of any society, even those that claim to have moved entirely past it.

## NOTES

1 Richard Kieckehefer, *Magic in the Middle Ages* (Cambridge: Cambridge University Press, 1989), 188; Owen Davies, "Magic in Common and Legal Perspectives," in *The Cambridge History of Magic and Witchcraft in the West: From Antiquity to the Present*, ed. David. J. Collins (Cambridge: Cambridge University Press, 2015), 521–46, at 536–37.

2 Herodotus, *Histories* 7.191; translation from *The Landmark Herodotus: The Histories*, trans. Andrea L. Purvis, ed. Robert B. Strassler (New York: Pantheon, 2007).

3 Pliny, *Natural History* 28.3–5; translations here and below are, with some modification, from *Natural History*, trans. William Henry Samuel Jones, vol. 8 (Cambridge, MA: Harvard University Press, 1963).

4 Pliny, *Natural History* 28.12.

5 Pliny, *Natural History* 28.23.

6 Augustine, *De doctrina Christiana* 2.20(31), ed. Joseph Martin, Corpus Christianorum Series Latina 32 (Turnhout: Brepols, 1962).

7 Translation from Alan Charles Kors and Edward Peters, eds., *Witchcraft in Europe 400–1700: A Documentary History*, 2nd ed. (Philadelphia: University of Pennsylvania Press, 2001), 62.

8 Bert Hansen, *Nicole Oresme and the Marvels of Nature: A Study of His "De causis mirabilium" with Critical Edition, Translation, and Commentary* (Toronto, ON: Pontifical Institute of Medieval Studies, 1985), 136.

9 Travis Zadeh, "Magic, Marvel, and Miracle in Early Islamic Thought," in *Magic and Witchcraft in the West*, 235–67, at 242–45.

10 Gideon Bohak, "Jewish Magic in the Middle Ages," in *Magic and Witchcraft in the West*, 268–99, at 275.

11 See Thomas S. Kuhn, *The Copernican Revolution: Planetary Astronomy in the Development of Western Thought* (Cambridge, MA: Harvard University Press, 1957), 131.

12 Leibniz's letters to Samuel Clarke, 4:45 and 5:35; Henry Gavin Alexander, ed., *The Leibniz-Clarke Correspondence* (Manchester: Manchester University Press, 1956), 43, 66.

13 Diderot, *Pensées philosophiques*, 12.

14 Peter Geschiere, *The Modernity of Witchcraft: Politics and the Occult in Postcolonial Africa*, trans. Peter Geschiere and Janet Roitman (Charlottesville: University of Virginia Press, 1997), 5–6, 169–70.

15 Margot Adler, *Drawing Down the Moon: Witches, Druids, Goddess-Worshippers, and Other Pagans in America Today*, 2nd ed. (New York: Penguin/Arkana, 1986), 112.

16  E.g. the film *The Craft* (1996) or the "Dark Willow" storyline in season six of *Buffy the Vampire Slayer* (2002).

17  Adam Ashforth, *Witchcraft, Violence, and Democracy in South Africa* (Chicago, IL: University of Chicago Press, 2005), 52–54; Peter Geschiere, *Witchcraft, Intimacy, and Trust: Africa in Comparison* (Chicago, IL: University of Chicago Press, 2013), 4.

18  Maarit Forde and Diana Paton, "Introduction," in *Obeah and Other Powers: The Politics of Caribbean Religion and Healing*, eds. Maarit Forde and Diana Paton (Durham, NC: Duke University Press, 2012), 26.

19  Patricia Birman, "Sorcery, Territories, and Marginal Resistance in Rio de Janeiro," in *Sorcery in the Black Atlantic*, eds. Luis Nicolau Parés and Roger Sansi (Chicago, IL: University of Chicago Press, 2011), 214–19; Geschiere, *Witchcraft, Intimacy, and Trust*, 202.

20  Bohak, "Jewish Magic," 270.

21  Zadeh, "Magic, Marvel, and Miracle in Early Islamic Thought," 248.

22  Derek Collins, *Magic in the Ancient Greek World* (Oxford: Blackwell, 2008), 134.

23  Collins, *Magic in the Ancient Greek World*, 35.

24  Collins, *Magic in the Ancient Greek World*, 159–60.

25  Alicia Walker, "Magic in Medieval Byzantium," in *Magic and Witchcraft in the West*, 210–11.

26  Philip A. Kuhn, *Soulstealers: The Chinese Sorcery Scare of 1768* (Cambridge, MA: Harvard University Press, 1990), 85–89.

27  Steve A. Smith, "Talking Toads and Chinless Ghosts: The Politics of 'Superstitious' Rumors in the People's Republic of China, 1961–1965," *American Historical Review* 111 (2006): 405–27.

28  See Kate Ramsey, *The Spirits and the Law: Vodou and Power in Haiti* (Chicago, IL: University of Chicago Press, 2011).

29  Ashforth, *Witchcraft, Violence, and Democracy*, 261–62.

30  Code of Hammurabi §2, translation from Robert Francis Harper, *The Code of Hammurabi, King of Babylon* (Chicago, IL: University of Chicago Press, 1904).

31  The history of magic in Europe, and particularly the history of witchcraft, is extremely well studied. Reliable overviews, on which I draw here, include Brian P. Levack, *The Witch-Hunt in Early Modern Europe*, 4th ed. (London: Routledge, 2016); Brian P. Levack, ed., *The Oxford Handbook of Witchcraft in Early Modern Europe and Colonial America* (Oxford: Oxford University Press, 2013).

32  Wolfgang Behringer, *Witches and Witch-Hunts: A Global History* (Cambridge: Polity Press, 2004), 130, 150.

# MAGICAL IDENTITIES

Anyone can practice magic. As I emphasized particularly in Chapter 2, while there are some highly elaborate forms of magic that require lengthy study and considerable resources to master, there are also innumerable common forms of magic – brief incantations, protective gestures, simple rites – that people can use without any specialized knowledge or claim to power. In societies in which most people believe in the real efficacy of magical acts, such practices are typically employed by the majority, at least on occasion. Then there are people who use magic more than just occasionally, and who are specifically identified as magicians (or sorcerers, or witches, or cunning-folk, or whatever). Such an identification can stem from their own claims, or it can be directed against them by suspicious neighbors. Sometimes it can float by in a whispered rumor, and sometimes it can come down thunderously in a legal pronouncement. People may embrace this identity, whether they have chosen it for themselves or not, or they may deny it resolutely. On certain bleak occasions throughout human history, people have denied the magical identity placed upon them literally with their dying breaths.

In some cases, being a magician can be a job description. I don't just mean modern stage magicians. In many cultures, self-identified magicians have earned their keep through their magical arts. Those who claim special abilities to heal, or divine hidden information, or communicate with spirits can provide services that many people want and for which they are willing to pay. And human nature being what it is, some people eagerly employ magical experts to direct curses or inflict harm on enemies or rivals. In classical antiquity, the similarity and almost standardization of many so-called curse tablets found around the Mediterranean indicate that they were often produced by at least quasi-professionals operating according to widely known guidelines. The curses they produced could then be used for anything from silencing a rival litigant in a legal proceeding to hobbling the horses of an opposing racing team in the hippodrome. In the modern Western world, an American anthropologist who apprenticed as a sorcerer in West Africa found that, as soon as his studies became known to his neighbors, people came to him seeking help against their enemies. He once prepared a spell for a friend whose cousin had been fired by his European boss. That man was not harmed directly, but less than a month after the spell was cast his sister became serious ill, so he had to leave his business and return to Europe for her treatment.[1]

What I mean by a magical identity, of course, runs far deeper than just hanging up a shingle and offering arcane services until quitting-time. If magic can, on occasion, be a way to earn a living, it is far more often a way of life. As the anthropologist mentioned above, Paul Stoller, revealed in his account of his apprenticeship, those who study magic among the Songhay people of Niger enter onto a distinct path. Unless they choose to step back off that path at some point (as he did), they will forever be marked, for good and for ill, as a sorcerer. In many cultures, while some kinds of magic are indeed learned skills, very often there is also some aspect of being a magician that is intrinsic to people. Again, among the Songhay, for example, sorcerers learn incantations and how to work with plants and powders. But they also consume a special powder that then remains in their stomachs, altering and fortifying them in various ways. Across Africa, the notion that magic often resides as a physical substance in the magician's digestive tract is common, but different societies conceive of magic residing within particular people in various ways.

So what sort of people do others typically see as having special magical inclinations or abilities? In attempting to say something globally applicable about how magical identities are assigned, I will latch onto the well-worn anthropological category of "the other." If, as I have been arguing steadily throughout this book, among the essential features of magic are its incomprehensibility and un-certainty, then it only makes sense that people would most often attribute magic to those who are unlike themselves. Members of other political or religious communities would be most obvious, but in fact, we more often find magic attributed to "others" within a given community: the socially marginal or outcast. I'll quickly complicate that idea, however, by noting how often magic can be attributed to close friends, neighbors, or family. In those cases, I'll assert, it represents the even more terrifying "other" within the heart of the familiar.

The central sections of this chapter will address the critically important issue of magic and gender. While it's far from true, for example, that all witches are women, the degree to which women have been associated with malevolent magic in many cultures is significant enough that it calls out for some attempt at explanation. Beyond witchcraft, there are other forms of magic, helpful as well as harmful, that have often carried a particularly feminine tinge, and I will also touch on these. Then, to balance the scales, I'll look at forms of magic typically associated with men and explore the gendered character of those practices as well. In conclusion, I will examine some of the reasons why people have either sought out an identity as a magician or at least accepted it when it has been ascribed to them. Because of the uneven power dynamics between men and women throughout most of human history, I will hazard the statement that more men have claimed to be magicians while more women have been accused of magical activities, but the analysis in this last section will not be driven primarily by gender.

## THE MAGIC OF OTHERS

Outright foreignness is by no means always a defining feature of magic. While for the ancient Greeks the original "magicians" were Persian priests, there were soon plenty of home-grown Hellenic *magoi* as well. Nevertheless, from antiquity onwards, certain lands and peoples have been more associated with magic than others. Astounding in its ancientness, even to other ancient cultures, Egypt was for many centuries a magical land *par excellence*. In the second century CE, Lucian of Samosata wrote, in Greek, about the powerful magician Pancrates, "versed in all the lore of the Egyptians," who spent more than two decades living in underground tombs at Memphis learning "occult sciences" directly from the goddess

Isis.[2] Roman opponents of Christianity sometimes alleged that Jesus had studied magic during his upbringing in Egypt, where the holy family fled from Herod's persecution. Christians objected, of course, but not because they denied Egypt's magical character. When one of the fathers of the church, Saint Jerome, wrote the life of the earlier Saint Hilarion in 390 CE, he included a story about a young man from Gaza who yearned for a chaste Christian girl. When his efforts to woo her failed, he traveled to Memphis and studied magic there for over a year. Upon his return, he buried "certain magical formulas and monstrous figures engraved on a thin sheet of Cyprian copper" under the threshold of the girl's house. She went mad with desire for him, forcing her parents to turn to the services of the saint, who miraculously cured her.[3]

Within Greece, the region of Thessaly was strongly associated with witchcraft. The first century CE Roman writer Lucan described Thessaly as a land forsaken by the gods and home to witches "surpassed by no invented horror / of a free imagination." In his account, not just the inhabitants but the landscape itself teemed with evil magic:

> On its crags the land of Thessaly produced / both harmful herbs and stones which hear magicians / chanting dreadful secrets. There arises many a substance / which puts constraint upon the gods: and in Haemonian lands / the Colchian stranger [the witch Medea] gathered herbs she had not brought with her.[4]

In medieval Europe, Christians often suspected Jews of possessing special affinity for magic, both because of their obvious (to Christian minds) entanglement with demons and their knowledge of Hebrew, an ancient and therefore magically powerful language. Muslims too were held suspect, and with some reason, given the number of magical texts that flowed into Western Europe from more intellectually advanced Muslim lands during Europe's so-called "renaissance of the twelfth century." Many such texts migrated through Iberia, where shifting boundaries of Christian and Muslim political control, along with a large Jewish population, produced a cultural mix that was strange and worrisome to many. For centuries, legends circulated of secret magical schools in Iberian lands, often presided over by the devil. Gerbert of Aurillac, a monk and important scholar who later reigned as Pope Sylvester II (999–1003), studied mathematics south of the Pyrenees, albeit in Christian controlled regions. By the eleventh century, a story had developed that he had learned magic there, which he used to advance his position in the church.

As Europeans extended their control over other regions of the globe in the early modern period, they tended to see magic in native practices wherever they went. Initially, this stemmed from the non-Christian nature of these practices, which European conquerors interpreted as demonic. Moving into the modern period, as European elites congratulated themselves on their progressive disenchantment and scientific rationality, they consequently tended to regard indigenous peoples as mired in various stages of primitive superstition, from which it was part of the "white man's burden" to liberate them. Within Europe, political and intellectual elites could also look with contempt on their own populations, seeing folk-practices as perhaps ethnographically interesting but also as signs of a superstitious primitivism that needed correction. In all cases, the association of certain peoples with magic served to distance and differentiate them from those who ruled over them, and in large part to justify that rule.

Although people often associate magic with foreignness, however, even more typically they find it close at hand, among members of their own communities. These are magicians to whom one can turn when in need of immediate help, and they also become the focus of immediate fears when there is some indication that magical harm has been wrought. The major witch hunts that took place in early modern Europe have provided scholars with the richest base of evidence through which to explore how magical beliefs and practices, or just the suspicion of these, operate in the context of relatively small, tightly knit communities.

Of course, individual cases vary in an almost infinite number of ways, but still, some basic patterns can be discerned. Trial records from across Europe reveal that accused witches were most typically old at the time of accusation, but that suspicions or even the firm local conviction that someone was a witch often extended back years. In other words, people usually lived with witches as their neighbors, often relying on them, however fretfully, for magical services until some event finally precipitated a formal accusation and trial.[5] Those identified as witches were usually not chosen at whim based on some fleeting grudge. Rather, they frequently appear to have violated social norms in some sustained way. For example, in the patriarchal society of the early modern period, unmarried adult women, whether spinsters or widows, represented a problem to social order just by their very existence, especially if they controlled wealth and might intrude on the smooth settling of inheritances from father to son.[6] Women who were perceived as "unruly" in any fashion – those who cursed, or didn't regularly attend church, or publically dominated their husbands, or constantly fought with their neighbors – might also become easy targets for accusation.

The poor of either gender could present a social problem, particularly if they did not confine themselves to what was perceived to be their proper place in society. Some classic analyses of European witchcraft associate accusations with social tensions arising from poor neighbors making what were perceived as excessive demands for charity within their community.[7] One highly influential analysis of the famous Salem trials in colonial New England demonstrated that most of the accusers came from the more mercantile-oriented Salem-Town, while most of the accused were from the more traditional/agricultural Salem-Village.[8] That is a highly particular dynamic that could not be expected to apply directly to other situations, but it serves to demonstrate yet another way in which those accused of being witches were perceived as somehow socially "other" by those who accused them.

Of course, we need to be careful about pressing any such sweeping argument too far. A recent trend in anthropological studies of witchcraft is for scholars to advance the counter-argument that suspicions and accusations need not operate by any clear social logic, nor function as a response to any discernable social stress.[9] Moreover, witchcraft is just one variety of magic, and people identified in their communities as magical experts need not be accused of being witches. In Europe, while traditional healers or cunning-folk might run afoul of zealous authorities who were convinced that any type of magic had to be demonic, within their communities they could be well-regarded and respectable. Although here too, one finds that healers, diviners, or other magicians who otherwise adhered closely to social norms fared better that those who did not.

Moreover, since most of these people claimed their identity openly, rather than confronting it as an accusation, it was this very assertion of special magical prowess that set them somewhat apart from their neighbors.

While historians of European witchcraft have focused on social dynamics within communities, anthropologists working in Africa have located the fear of witches arising in an even tighter social setting, within families and households. The underlying concern here seems to be that those closest to oneself might not be as they appear, and might not act as they are supposed to. In the words of Peter Geschiere, witchcraft accusations among kin represent "the frightening realization that there is jealousy and therefore aggression within the family, where there should be only trust and solidarity."[10]

Further along this trajectory, and even more terrifying than the suspicion that one's neighbors or kin could be malevolent magicians, is the fact that in some societies witches are thought not just to mask their evil natures but to be entirely unaware of them. Here a perceived affinity for magic becomes, in effect, otherness hidden within oneself. Historically, Europe knew this dynamic after a fashion. Throughout the period of major trials, both religious and judicial authorities maintained that witches and other magicians had been seduced by the devil, and the devil was, of course, the father of lies (John 8:44). Presuming many accused witches were people who might have engaged in magical healing, divination, or other such rites, authorities sometimes alleged that they simply did not understand the true demonic nature of their activities. In fact, however, the most basic structures of European witch-hunting presumed that people knew that they were diabolical witches and just lied about it in court, hence the frequent recourse to torture to wring the truth from them.

In other parts of the world, the insidious nature of witchcraft could be far more profound. As I've mentioned at several points already, in many African and Asian societies witchcraft is believed to be a physical substance that comes to reside within a person, often lodging in the stomach. In such cases, witches may or may not realize that they have this substance inside them, or, if they have it, they may not know if it has been activated in some way to make them a witch. In his classic study of witchcraft among the East-African Azande, E. E. Evans-Pritchard noted the belief that people could be witches and perform acts of maleficent magic entirely unknowingly.[11] In a more recent study, Nils Bubandt has identified a similar dynamic in Indonesia. Witches there are ferocious creatures who devour the livers of their victims. Neither witches nor victims, however, have any memory of these attacks, for the magic involved closes all wounds and causes both parties to forget. Victims will typically grow ill and waste away, but only when they are on the point of death will they remember the attack and perhaps identify the witch who assailed them. Even amidst such extreme uncertainty, however, signals exist that can indicate a possible witch, and here too these have to do with a person failing to conform to accepted social norms, particularly by demonstrating excessive stinginess, greed, arrogance, or disrespect.[12]

## WISE WOMEN AND WICKED WITCHES

Whenever magical identities carry negative associations, it only makes sense that they would more easily be ascribed to people who demonstrate some degree of social "deviance," however that might be perceived, and we can extend this argument to the realm of gender. In many societies, traditionally male behavior and even the male body have been taken as normative, with female behavior and physicality therefore categorized as "other." Likewise, in many societies, and certainly in Western society from antiquity onwards, various kinds of magic, and especially negative and harmful magic, have been associated with women. Yet, no society identifies all woman as pernicious practitioners of harmful magic. Witch-hunting has never amounted simply to woman-hunting, and even in Europe at the height of the early modern trials, accusations of witchcraft were not "sex-specific," although obviously in many places they were "sex-related."[13]

Let's begin, therefore, with a couple of caveats, before delving all too briefly into this complex topic. First, although I'll continue to draw heavily on studies of European witchcraft in this section because that is the area in which the most gender-focused research on magic has been done, I don't mean to imply that even European society, let alone others, identifies female magic exclusively with harmful magic. Women may just as often be particularly adept at healing, amorous or reproductive magic, or divination. Second, although I will be suggesting that some magical practices could be perceived as more female or feminine, at no point do I mean to imply that any major forms of magic were ever associated exclusively with women. Staying with European witchcraft as the example, 75 percent of those executed during the period of major witch trials were women, but that still leaves 25 percent who were men. Also, in certain regions (e.g. Normandy, Iceland, parts of Scandinavia, and all of Russia), the majority of convicted witches were men. With these exceptions and reservations being noted, however, the point here is to ask, when certain kinds of magic have been associated more strongly with women than with men, how that magical identity relates to gender identity.

To begin with those situations in which the assertion of a magical identity comes in the form of a legal accusation and becomes a matter for a legal ruling, women may be more vulnerable by virtue of the fact that in many societies they are more legally vulnerable in general than men are, or at least they occupy a more precarious or dependent legal position. Again, the obvious example comes from witch trials in early modern Europe, although courts in that period could also try women (and men) for lesser magical crimes: illicit healing, herbalism, love magic, or divination. Not as much research has focused on these other areas, but from witch trials alone, the general shape of women's plight is clear. On average, they were more likely to be accused of a magical crime than were men, once accused they were more likely to be convicted, and once convicted they were more likely to be executed rather than face some less severe punishment.

An important factor behind this disparity was that, in most jurisdictions across much of this period, women had little or no independent legal standing. That is, their ability to mount any defense depended on the willingness of male relatives or other protectors to come to their aid. In many cases, the women mostly likely to be swept up in witch trials were precisely those who lacked any male defenders. Elderly spinsters or widows, for example, might have no close male relatives or none who cared much about them. Worse still, male relatives could sometimes see a widow in the family as an impediment to speedy or direct male inheritance. Given the near-infinite permutations possible in witchcraft accusations, men could find any number of reasons for leaving their women in the witchcraft lurch. Nevertheless, it clearly will not do to argue that women faced more frequent prosecution as witches solely because they made better legal targets. If so, we would expect to see gender imbalances in many other crimes tried by these same courts. We should also be ready to accept the possibility that in many societies, women are thought to perform certain types of magic more than men either because they, in fact, do so or at least because their society perceives some major kinds of magic as pertaining to decidedly female areas of activity.

In many premodern societies, a tremendous amount of what I discussed in Chapter 2 as common or low magic, the sort of practices that people might employ during everyday activities, has to do with fertility. This can mean human fertility and can entail magic to aid in sexual activity and conception, or rites that can hinder such activity, or spells or potions that serve as an abortifacient if an unwanted conception has occurred. Such magic can also involve rites to ensure the health of both mother and baby during childbirth or to promote the healthy development of children in their early years. Around the world, for obvious reasons, reproduction and childbirth have very typically been the domain of women, and so the magic that pertains to that domain can become the special province of women. Naturally, this does not apply to all situations, and men can certainly obsess about their sexual performance as well, but I'll note some gendered distinctions that scholars have observed in love magic below.

The issue of fertility can also extend to the health and fecundity of domestic animals, which are frequently under the care of women in many traditional agricultural societies, while men work in the fields. Women also often tend domestic-scale gardens or gather roots and plants, again while men work fields or pastures, and so the magic of plants and herbs is, sometimes, associated strongly with women. Rites used to protect the fertility of crops in the fields, on the other hand, may be more easily associated with men. In medieval Europe, for example, male representatives of that most patriarchal of institutions, the Catholic Church, regularly processed with a consecrated Eucharist around fields to ensure a good harvest, and bishops would sometimes formally exorcise fields to drive out harmful insects and vermin. Women are, however, often seen as harming crops. European witches were commonly thought to destroy crops either by bringing some form of pestilence or by conjuring destructive storms. Interesting and perhaps indicative of some of the gendered perceptions of such magical practices is that in early modern Russia, where accused witches were mostly men, almost no charges of weather magic appear in the trial records.[14]

European witches were also widely suspected of preventing conception in women, or killing and eating young children after they were born, and they also supposedly attacked male virility, sometimes literally causing the male member to vanish. The *Malleus Maleficarum* went so far as to claim that witches stored their stolen penises in large chests or sometimes in birds' nests in the trees.[15] Love magic, designed to arouse or destroy amorous desire or sexual capability, can be associated either with women or with men, but there may well be a particularly female form of love magic apparent in many diverse cultures. Rather than aggressive, "masculine" spells intended to enthrall an unwilling lover, it involves what can be characterized as defensive spells used to ward off sexual rivals. Scholars of Greco-Roman antiquity have argued that women used such magic not directly for amorous reasons, out of jealousy or sexual desire, but to protect their social and economic status, which for respectable matrons depended almost entirely on their marital relationship.[16] Similar magic still exists millennia later. In modern North America, the African-American conjure tradition offers many rites to "hoodoo a man's nature," sometimes simply to harm him, but often to ensure fidelity.[17] Likewise, so-called knot-spells for binding a man's sexuality are known across Africa as well.

Moving beyond fertility and reproduction, women are frequently associated with domestic duties like cooking, and are often the first caregivers to the sick, before a more professional healer, possibly male or female, might be brought in. Cooking is a necessary but also a perilous task, and a cook can easily fall under suspicion of poisoning if someone sickens or dies after eating certain foods. As we've seen several times already, many cultures have considered poisoning to be a form of magical harm. Likewise dealing with the sick can be risky business. Obviously, an illness might worsen rather than improve under treatment. But even when a sick person gets better, the suspicion can persist that those who know how to heal also know how to harm.

Much had been made of male medical authorities using accusations of magic or witchcraft to undermine particularly female areas of medical knowledge or care, but arguments here can become tenuous. For example, the idea that male physicians used charges of witchcraft against female midwives in early modern Europe has largely been demolished by careful research. In fact, midwives were usually respected for their craft, including their knowledge of rites used to protect mother and child from witches.[18] Nevertheless, as I've reiterated several times, medicine and magic do blur together in many societies. Rather than arguing that women healers run a greater risk than men of being identified as magicians or witches, I'd suggest that any healer without clear professional credentials runs such a risk, and in most societies, those credentials have been bestowed primarily or exclusively on men.

By highlighting the connections between certain kinds of magical practices and what have traditionally been regarded in many societies as female activities, I am not naively asserting that most accused witches or other women associated with magic necessarily performed the magic of which they were accused, merely that structures existed in their societies that allowed people (men and women) to more easily believe that women might be specially inclined to certain types of magic. Such cultural perceptions, whether grounded in any reality or not, are undoubtedly the most powerful reason for the gender associations that pertain to certain magical identities. Such connections, however, are more complex than they might at first appear, and they can function in some surprising ways.

Throughout history, Western cultures have positioned women as inferior to men in multiple ways: intellectual, morally, physically, and spiritually. The connection between such stereotypes and the predominance of women accused of witchcraft can appear self-evident. Toward the end of the fifteenth century, the *Malleus Maleficarum* infamously proclaimed that "all witchcraft comes from carnal lust, which in women in insatiable."[19] Nearly fifteen hundred years earlier, the Jewish sage Hillel declared, "more women, more witchcraft."[20] Older still is the terse injunction in Exodus 22:18, rendered in the King James Bible as "Thou shalt not suffer a witch to live." The original Hebrew did indeed use a female term, *mekhashefah* (the verse is 22:17 in the Tanakh), but the proper implication to be drawn from this brief passage is much debated, and it is frequently contrasted to other more extensive injunctions, such as Deuteronomy 18:9–11, which utilizes the male term *mekashef* and so indicates that men, as well as women, could be associated with forbidden magic.

Many ancient Near-eastern cultures imagined a fearsome female demon that prowled the night, inflicting illness and injury. Called Lilitu in Babylon and Assyria, she became Lilith for the Hebrews, and as her image moved down the centuries it helped to inspire enduring stereotypes of night-stalking witches. Classical Western literature, especially from the Roman period, also contains horrific images of female witches. Bloodthirsty Medea murders her own children, and horrible Erictho performs grisly rites with bits of corpses snatched from pyres, gallows, crosses, and fresh graves. She lives amidst tombs, and when she emerges, "she tramples and she scorches up the seeds of fertile corn / and with breath corrupts the breezes not fatal before."[21] Such descriptions were purely literary, and trials records and artifacts of magic, such as curse tablets that name both victims and users, point to men engaging in harmful magic as much as women in classical antiquity. Yet, images have their own power, and ancient literature became an important source from which later European societies drew their stereotypes of witches and women.

Stereotypes need not be simple, however, or forever fixed. In addition to maleficent magic, women in Western antiquity were often depicted as having special oracular powers, and in medieval Europe, too, women were sometimes presented as more prone to divine inspiration and mystical visions than were men, precisely because they were thought to be less intelligent, less rational, and more susceptible to spiritual impressions. Such characteristics, unfortunately, also rendered them more vulnerable to demonic possession and the deceptions of the devil, but those female mystics who could convince male authorities of their veracity could be highly respected and achieve a kind of authority themselves over the men around them. In the modern West, women figured prominently as mediums and clairvoyants in the nineteenth-century spiritualist revival, and in the twentieth century, explicitly feminist strains of modern Witchcraft may celebrate women's affinity for magic, still based in part on such (formerly negative) stereotypes as their being less strictly rational and more in tune with nature than men are. Even long-accursed Lilith has gone from being a night-stalking monster to a symbol of female empowerment.

Around the world, gender interacts with magical identities in complex ways. Among the Azande of East Africa, witches could be either men or women, but while men could be bewitched by either sex, women were thought primarily to be victims of other women practicing witchcraft. Also, women rarely become witch-doctors.[22] Among the Yoruba people, witchcraft is thought to be equally common among men and women, but women accused of being witches are treated more harshly.[23] In Central and South America, it can be difficult to identify clear pre-colonial cultural norms, but we can observe some curious responses to colonial impositions. In Peru, for example, after the Spanish conquest, many native women accommodated themselves to the magical identities that their colonial rulers placed upon them, including a proclivity for diabolical witchcraft. But among their fellow natives, these "witches" became highly respected figures, as "witchcraft, maintenance of ancient traditions, and conscious political resistance became increasingly intertwined for colonial Indians."[24] In colonial Mexico, Spanish women sometimes interacted with Indians in a kind of magical sub-culture, exchanging or purchasing spells, powders, and other magical material, since male colonial authorities asserted that both groups shared an inclination for such practices anyway.[25]

## THE MALE MAGUS

Wherever Europeans established colonial dominance, they tried to transplant their cultural norms, and this included imposing ideas of who might perform magic. Native women maintaining traditional rites became witches, as might native men, although they were more strongly associated with other forms of magical superstition. Here gendered thinking combined with racism. As European women were held to be intellectually and morally inferior to men, so all indigenous peoples were regarded as intellectual and morally inferior to Europeans, and thus more prone to magic. This stereotype endured well into the era of modern imperialism.

But lest we forget, there were male witches within Europe too. Up to a quarter of all accusations during the period of the early modern witch hunts were directed against men, and this percentage would grow substantially if other cases involving charges of super-stitious magic that fell below the threshold of diabolical witchcraft were included. Some scholars have argued that men suspected of witchcraft either displayed feminine behavior or found themselves being feminized in the course of their trials.[26] Others maintain that male suspects may have violated social norms, but not in parti-cularly feminized ways. That is, they behaved like reprobate men, but not like women.[27] Then there are the regions within Europe where witches were predominantly male. In early-modern Russia, for example, the gender ratio in witch trials was almost the exact opposite of that in Western Europe, with 74 percent men and only 26 percent women among the accused.[28] The current best analysis is that in Russia's fiercely hierarchical society, people turned to magic, especially harmful magic, when they felt they had been wronged by a superior against whom they could not otherwise gain redress. Western Europe had its hierarchies as well, and under nor-mal circumstances, only a very foolish peasant or lowly craftsman would bring charges of witchcraft against a noblewoman. But Russian society was even more severely gradated, with fewer pro-tections limiting superiors from heaping abuse on their inferiors, so gender divisions simply played a lesser role in the overall social framework of magic.[29]

The gendering of magical identities differed not just in certain zones of the Western world, but also at certain times. During the first few centuries of Christianity, while church fathers some-times decried the magical practices of women, they targeted men, particularly the leaders of powerful rival movements within the new faith that needed to be crushed. Historically, there has never been a single Christianity, but rather contending groups claiming inspiration from, and arguing over the correct interpretation of, the figure of Jesus. As the early structures of Christianity took shape, and as certain interpretations gained dominance, others were cast by emerging church authorities as heresies, and the leaders of these groups were often condemned as demonically inspired magicians. The figure of Simon Magus, literally Simon the Magician, became the model. He is presented briefly as a wizard and opponent of the apostle Simon Peter in the Acts of the Apostles (8:9–24) but re-ceives much greater coverage in the influential, albeit apocryphal,

Acts of Peter. The New Testament and other early Christian texts contain many other descriptions of (male) disciples of Christ confronting male magicians, in which contests of supernatural power overlay deeper contestations of social and intellectual authority.

For the rest of Christian history, the learned male magus might be castigated by clerical authorities as engaging in demonic magic, but he cut a very different figure from that of the lowly witch, or indeed any practitioner, male or female, of simple common magic. In medieval Europe, men specializing in complex ritual magic used arcane texts to invoke spiritual powers. Sometimes they conceived of the entities they invoked as angelic and sometimes as explicitly demonic (these beings were always demons to suspicious authorities), but the nature of their practices spoke to their intelligence, education, and dominating will, not to their subjugation as servants of the devil. The great age of the male magus was in Europe's early modern period, however, when some leading Renaissance intellectuals turned to magic, working out new systems of occult thought in accordance with Neoplatonic philosophy, Jewish Kabbalistic theories, or putatively ancient Hermeticism (referring to a body of texts associated with the mythic figure of Hermes Trismegistus, supposedly an Egyptian sage who predated Plato and even Moses, although the earliest Hermetic works actually date to within a few centuries of the time of Christ). Likewise, astrologers and alchemists considered themselves masters of learned, scientific crafts, deserving respect for their erudition.

These systems of magic, intellectually ornate and often deliberately obscure, with pseudo-histories that stretched almost to the dawn of time, inspired later occult movements that, while sometimes proving quite open to women, were dominated by men. The most famous modern occultist group was the Hermetic Order of the Golden Dawn, founded in Britain in the late nineteenth century, although based in part on earlier Masonic structures. Other groups existed even earlier, such as the Martinist Order in France, founded by Louis-Claude de Saint-Martin in the late eighteenth century and based on the teachings of Martinès de Pasqually, who himself had established an occult order of Elus Coën, or Elect Priests, in the mid-1700s. Most of these groups had a certain air of male clubbiness to them, and for many of their solidly middle- and upper-class members, they were just a diverting pastime. For the committed few, however, their magical systems stressed arcane learning, the strength of the magician's will, and in some cases serious rivalry and competitions for power.

Elsewhere in the modern world magic and magicians very much operate in traditionally masculine realms of political and economic competition and power. In many parts of Africa, for example, politicians regularly employ magicians to influence the public and attack their rivals. One expert has provocatively compared these political witch-doctors to Western political spin-doctors, arguing that politicians use them to achieve the same ends.[30] Other kinds of magicians engage with modern economic dynamics. I've already mentioned, for example, how in Cameroon a new kind of witch-craft known as *nyongo* has developed, which involves using spells to create a zombie labor force instead of killing victims outright. "*Nyongo* men" can be recognized by their sudden new wealth and their ability to profit from modern economic structures in what appear to many to be mysterious and occult ways.[31] Similarly in the early twentieth century in Haiti, rumors appear to have circulated about zombie labor being used by HASCO, the Haytian American Sugar Company.[32] Returning to Africa, young conmen who profit from various, thoroughly modern black market activities are often regarded as magicians as well.[33]

Magic's connection to the traditionally male world of warfare and combat has been surprisingly little studied. Magical weapons abound in mythologies of most cultures, and commanders through-out history have resorted to astrology or divination to determine the best time to engage in a battle. In modern times, as I've already mentioned in Chapter 2, both Boxer rebels in China and Zulu warriors in South Africa turned to magical rites that they believed would protect them from the bullets of their European foes. Even more recently, during the civil war in Mozambique in the 1970s and 1980s, traditional magicians enchanted rebel troops to make them invulnerable to bullets. The government proclaimed such magic to be empty superstition, but there is evidence that more than a few government troops also availed themselves of traditional protective rites. Likewise, in Sierra Leone's civil war during the 1990s, magicians offered combatants the advantages not only of invulnerability but also of invisibility.[34]

## CHOOSING MAGIC

So far in this chapter, I have been focusing mainly, although not exclusively, on situations in which magical identities have been applied to certain people by others, sometimes through community rumor and gossip and sometimes through legal proceedings. Many people choose to pursue and practice magic, however, deliberately claiming it as part of their identity. Others split the difference, appropriating and developing their identity as magicians after it has been ascribed to them. In this final section, I'll explore why they might make this sometimes dangerous choice.

Magic has always been alluring, promising arcane knowledge and occult power. One of its great attractions is the intellectual enticement of the mysterious. Among the best examples of magicians who have pursued their art out of pure intellectual curiosity would be the Renaissance mages of early modern Europe, mentioned above. Men like Marsilio Ficino (1433–1499), Giovanni Pico della Mirandola (1463–1494), Cornelius Agrippa von Nettesheim (1486–1535), Paracelsus (1494–1541), John Dee (1527–1608), and Giordano Bruno (1548–1600) are remembered as humanists, philosophers, and scientists as much as, and in some cases more than, they are as magicians. They all explored occult and mystical systems in an effort to understand the universe better, and they frequently studied astrology and alchemy, which remained fully integrated into the natural philosophy, that is, the natural science, of their day.

Although Europe's Scientific Revolution is often thought to have marked an important step toward so-called disenchantment, we've also seen how many leading early scientific figures had significant magical credentials on their resumes. It bears remembering that even so iconic an early modern scientist as Isaac Newton was deeply interested in alchemy, and he corresponded about the mysteries of that occult art with his friend and one of the leading political philosophers of the Enlightenment, John Locke. Similarly, European occultists of the eighteenth, nineteenth, and early twentieth centuries often considered themselves investigators into mysteries of both the physical universe and the human mind. Strong connections exist between occultism and the origins of modern psychology in this period, and occult interests are evident in the work of Sigmund Freud and even more so in that of Carl Jung. Centuries earlier, putatively pious monks preserved magical texts on the shelves of monastery libraries, it has been argued, because they used the rites contained in these works to explore the natural wonders of God's creation and to delve into the mysteries of spirituality and explore the nature of the divine itself.[35]

Aside from satisfying pure curiosity, developing special skills in the practice of magic has also often been a route to power – not just the direct power that magical rites themselves might promise, but access to political power. I've already mentioned how many politicians in modern Africa use the services of witch doctors, but political leaders having magicians in their employ is scarcely a new thing. Magical demimondes have been found to exist at aristocratic courts in both the ancient world and medieval Europe.[36] The presence of such people at court allowed rulers access to magical power, but the courtiers themselves also benefited. Usually of low rank, by claiming to possess special magical prowess, they created a space for themselves within otherwise inaccessible courtly hierarchies. These models of magical identity have been show to exist in varied political settings, as far afield as Imperial China.[37]

Of course, magicians serving at court or otherwise associated with ruling elites are often paid for their services or receive lucrative patronage in some form. Outside of the halls of political power, too, economic gain can be a strong incentive to claim an identity as a magician. In towns and villages across Europe, cunning-folk of various kinds frequently charged for their services, offering healing, divination, or protection from perceived harmful forms of magic for a price. When Western legal regimes decided that they no longer accepted the reality of magical practices, they stopped threatening such people with charges of diabolism and witchcraft and instead charged them with fraud for bilking others out of money by peddling impossible services. Across Africa, magicians can make a good living from their craft. A powerful sorcerer among the Songhay of Niger, for example, might sometimes charge the equivalent of $100 for a charm or amulet, which might exceed a year's income for some of her clients.[38] In and around the Caribbean, practitioners of Obeah, Vodou, and Santería may charge for services, or often, if they decline a formal payment, clients will leave what are characterized as "offerings" instead.[39]

Detailed research has shown how practices of *brujería* in Puerto Rico have adapted to fit within a modern consumer economy.[40]

Beyond simple financial reward, people may choose to adopt or embrace a magical identity for the social standing it can confer. Especially powerful or successful healers and diviners can achieve widespread reputations in Africa or the Caribbean, and in South American Candomblé, *mães* and *pais de santo* (literally mothers or fathers of a saint) are highly respected figures. As these names suggest, people whom others might label magicians, or even witches, can claim religious inspiration and validation. A powerful Puerto Rican *brujo* might assert that the Virgin Mary selected him for his calling, for example, while the early modern Italian *benandanti* identified by Carlo Ginzburg claimed that they were called by angels to battle evil witches in spirit form to defend the fertility of fields and ensure a good harvest.[41] When inquisitors from nearby Venice began to investigate, however, they quickly became convinced that the *benandanti* were themselves diabolical witches.

This shows how precarious a reputation tied to a magical identity can be. In Europe, Christian authorities proclaimed for centuries that there was no such thing as good magic, and all purported healers or diviners were in fact witches in league with the devil. Ordinary people rarely seem to have accepted the conflation of helpful and harmful magic absolutely, especially when they have found themselves to need magical assistance. Still, the reputation even of generally well-regarded cunning-folk could be fraught with peril. Given the necessarily mysterious power these magical experts claimed to wield, many people regarded them with at least some suspicion, even if they were not ready to declare them to be witches. Across Africa, too, healers and diviners are respected but also feared, for the magic that can heal may also harm. Moreover, the powerful voice of Western modernity now declares such people to be powerless quacks, while, in an eerie echo from the era of Europe's witch hunts, fundamentalist Christian (and Muslim) preachers are fanning out across the continent to proclaim them to be monstrously evil servants of the devil.

Still, clearly some people find that it is worth running such risks for the chance to obtain a certain standing in their communities, even if a potentially negative one, and to command fear if not admiration. Particularly for women in societies where other paths to significant social status are often reserved exclusively for men, a magical reputation may be quite attractive. Many studies have shown how the poor old women so typically suspected of being witches in early modern Europe sometimes embraced even that incredibly dangerous reputation. Precisely because they were poor, old, and female, and so in all other ways mostly despised by their communities, at least the suspicion of witchcraft gave them a certain dark aura. Perhaps they really believed they had magical powers. Most likely they did not believe that they worshiped demons, attended sabbaths, or any of the other more colorful accusations that could arise against them in court, but maybe in some cases they believed even that. Psychologically oriented histories have shown how readily people can internalize their societies' normative beliefs. And if it is normal to suspect that a poor woman who is often resentful of her better-to-do neighbors, or who doesn't display the proper signs of maternal care toward her children, or who feels lustful thoughts when she should be pure and virginal might well be a servant of the devil, no doubt some of those women honestly believed this about themselves as well.[42] For all that I've focused here on "practical" reasons why people might be motivated to fashion themselves into magicians, I do not mean to discount the simplest explanation: that they truly believe themselves to have the special knowledge, power, and talents that they claim.

Finally, although magicians must often accept a powerful but potentially negative or at least ambiguous reputation in their communities, many also pursue a magical identity because it can confer a sense of community all its own. We've already seen an example of this among the clubby occultists of nineteenth- and early-twentieth-century Europe, as they formed exclusive societies, orders, and confraternities of various kinds. One might also imagine, perhaps, a more attenuated sense of community among the learned mages of Renaissance Europe. Often in contact with one another at least through their writings and exploring arcane topics that many others, even among the intelligentsia, considered foolish or taboo, they comprised an occult clique within the larger Republic of Letters of their age. Likewise, it is clear that sorcerers in many African societies consider themselves members of a kind of elite group, even though they operate as individuals and may, in fact, be in rivalry with each other.

The most profound example of magical identity as a means to community, however, is the most recent: modern Witchcraft, also known as Wicca, along with other magically oriented neo-pagan movements that have developed since the mid-twentieth century. One scholar has even suggested that modern Witches are in fact emblematic of the modern condition, because only in the modern Western world can one truly "stand outside of time and tradition" and fashion one's own identity and sense of community with complete freedom.[43] Whether that is entirely true or not, modern Witchcraft is attractive to many of its practitioners not so much for the magical power it promises, but because it can be a means to fashion a new sense of self within a self-chosen community. Witches frequently take up that identity as teens or young adults, and this decision is obviously part of their process of separating themselves from or even rebelling against parental or family beliefs or traditions.

As the Wiccan movement has aged, it has itself become a traditional belief system for some, with children now being raised in the new religion of Witchcraft. Nevertheless, at least into the first decades of the twenty-first century, Wiccan and other neo-pagan identities still convey some level of deliberate rejection of mainstream Western religions and other value systems. Although many Witches practice as individuals, they still share at least some sense of community with each other through books and magazines, festivals and conventions, and of course now an endless number of internet websites. And many do practice in groups, which can become quite tight-knit, due in part to the fact that their members have chosen to step outside of their societies' mainstream together, and those societies still view them with certain lingering suspicions. In that sense, this most modern of magical identities is quite akin to that of other witches and magicians in the past.

## NOTES

1 Paul Stoller and Cheryl Olkes, *In Sorcery's Shadow: A Memoir of Apprenticeship among the Songhay of Niger* (Chicago, IL: University of Chicago Press, 1987), 110–18.

2 *The Works of Lucian of Samosata*, trans. Henry Watson Fowler and Francis George Fowler, 4 vols. (Oxford: Clarendon Press, 1905), 3:249.

3 Saint Jerome, *Vita Sancti Hilarionis* 21(23), in Jacques-Paul Migne, *Patrologia Latina* 23, cols. 347–420; I have slightly modified the translation in W. H. Fremantle, G. Lewis, and W. G. Martley, *Nicene and Post-Nicene Fathers*, second series, vol. 6, ed. Philip Schaff and Henry Wace (Buffalo, NY: Christian Literature Publishing Co., 1893).

4 Lucan, *De bello civili* 6.436–37 and 6.438–42; *The Civil War*, trans. Susan H. Braund (Oxford: Oxford University Press, 1992), 118.

5 Robin Briggs, *Witches and Neighbors: The Social and Cultural Context of European Witchcraft* (New York: Viking, 1996), is especially good on this point.

6 An important study here, dealing with the New World rather than the Old, is Carol F. Karlsen, *The Devil in the Shape of a Woman: Witchcraft in Colonial New England* (1987; reprint New York: Norton, 1998).

7 Alan Macfarlane, *Witchcraft in Tudor and Stuart England: A Regional and Comparative Study* (London: Routledge, 1970); Keith Thomas, *Religion and the Decline of Magic* (New York: Scribner's, 1971).

8 Paul Boyer and Stephen Nissenbaum, *Salem Possessed: The Social Origins of Witchcraft* (Cambridge, MA: Harvard University Press, 1974).

9 James Siegel, *Naming the Witch* (Stanford, CA: Stanford University Press, 2005); Nils Bubandt, *The Empty Seashell: Witchcraft and Doubt on an Indonesian Island* (Ithaca, NY: Cornell University Press, 2014).

10 Peter Geschiere, *The Modernity of Witchcraft: Politics and the Occult in Postcolonial Africa*, trans. Peter Geschiere and Janet Roitman (Charlottesville: University of Virginia Press, 1997), 11; more generally and with comparison to Europe see Peter Geschiere, *Witchcraft, Intimacy, and Trust: Africa in Comparison* (Chicago, IL: University of Chicago Press, 2013).

11 Edward Evan Evans-Pritchard, *Witchcraft, Oracles, and Magic among the Azande*, abridged ed. (Oxford: Clarendon, 1976), 58–59.

12 Bubandt, *Empty Seashell*, 193.

13 This terminology is from Christina Larner, *Witchcraft and Religion: The Politics of Popular Belief* (Oxford: Blackwell, 1984), 84–88.

14 Valerie Kivelson, *Desperate Magic: The Moral Economy of Witchcraft in Seventeenth-Century Russia* (Ithaca, NY: Cornell University Press, 2013), 79.

15 Heinrich Kramer, *Malleus Maleficarum* 2.1.7. For a cross-cultural analysis, see Moira Smith, "The Flying Phallus and the Laughing Inquisitor: Penis Theft in the *Malleus Maleficarum*," *Journal of Folklore Research* 39 (2002): 85–117.

16 David Frankfurter, "The Social Context of Women's Erotic Magic in Late Antiquity," in *Daughters of Hecate: Women and Magic in the Ancient World*, eds. Kimberly B. Stratton and Dayna S. Kalleres (Oxford: Oxford University Press, 2014), 319–39; Pauline Ripat, "Cheating Women: Curse Tablets and Roman Wives," in *Daughters of Hecate*, 340–64.

17 Smith, "Flying Phallus," 94–95; Yvonne P. Chireau, *Black Magic: Religion and the African American Conjuring Tradition* (Berkeley, University of California Press, 2003), 79–80.

18 David Harley, "Historians as Demonologists: The Myth of the Midwife-Witch," *Social History of Medicine* 3 (1990): 1–26

19 Kramer, *Malleus Maleficarum* 1.6.

20 *m. Avot* 2.7.

21 Lucan, *De bello civili* 6.521–22; translation from *The Civil War* (as n. 4 above), p. 120.

22 Evans-Pritchard, *Witchcraft*, 8, 72.

23 Elias Bongmba, "African Witchcraft: From Ethnography to Critique," in *Witchcraft Dialogues: Anthropological and Philosophical Exchanges*, eds. George Clement Bond and Diane M. Ciekawy (Athens: Ohio University Press, 2001), 53; Barry Hallen, "'Witches' as Superior Intellects: Challenging a Cross-Cultural Superstition," in *Witchcraft Dialogues*, 85–86.

24 Irene Silverblatt, *Moon, Sun, and Witches: Gender Ideologies and Class in Inca and Colonial Peru* (Princeton, NJ: Princeton University Press, 1987), 194–96.

25 Laura A. Lewis, *Hall of Mirrors: Power, Witchcraft, and Caste in Colonial Mexico* (Durham, NC: Duke University Press, 2003), 118–22.

26 Laura Apps and Andrew Gow, *Male Witches in Early Modern Europe* (Manchester: Manchester University Press, 2003).

27 Robin Briggs, "Male Witches in the Duchy of Lorraine," in *Witchcraft and Masculinities in Early Modern Europe*, ed. Alison Rowlands (Basingstoke: Palgrave Macmillan, 2009), 31–51; Jonathan Durrant, "Why Some Witches and Not Others? The Male Witches of Eichstätt," in *Witchcraft and Masculinities*, 100–120, makes a similar point.

28 Kivelson, *Desperate Magic*, 83.

29 Kivelson, *Desperate Magic*, passim.

30 Peter Geschiere, "On Witch Doctors and Spin Doctors: The Role of 'Experts' in African and American Politics," in *Magic and Modernity: Interfaces of Revelation and Concealment*, eds. Birgit Meyer and Peter Pels (Stanford, CA: Stanford University Press, 2003), 159–82.

31 Geschiere, *Modernity of Witchcraft*, 147–48.

32 Kate Ramsey, *The Spirits and the Law: Vodou and Power in Haiti* (Chicago, IL: University of Chicago Press, 2011), 172–76. Although this rumor was documented by occultist and travel-writer William B. Seabrook, Ramsey argues it is reasonable that Haitians could have thought of HASCO acting in this way; likewise Stephan Palmié, *The Cooking of History: How Not to Study Afro-Cuban Religion* (Chicago, IL: University of Chicago Press, 2013), 65.

33 Basile Ndjio, "Mokoagne moni: Sorcery and New Forms of Wealth in Cameroon," in *The Religion of Fools: Superstition Past and Present*, eds. S. A. Smith and Alan Knight (Oxford: Oxford University Press, 2008), 271–89.

34 Alcinda Honwana, "Undying Past: Spirit Possession and the Memory of War in Southern Mozambique," in *Magic and Modernity*, 60–80, at 67; and Rosalind Shaw, "Robert Kaplan and 'Juju Journalism' in Sierra Leone's Rebel War: The Primitivizing of an African Conflict," in *Magic and Modernity*, 81–102, at 81.

35 Sophie Page, *Magic in the Cloister: Pious Motives, Illicit Interests, and Occult Approaches to the Medieval Universe* (University Park: Pennsylvania State University Press, 2013).

36 Peter Brown, "Sorcery, Demons, and the Rise of Christianity from Late Antiquity to the Middle Ages," in *Witchcraft Confessions and Accusations*, ed. Mary Douglas (London: Routlege, 1970), 17–45, at 25–26; Edward Peters, *The Magician, the Witch, and the Law* (Philadelphia: University of Pennsylvania Press, 1978), 112–25.

37 Xiaohuan Zhao, "Political Uses of Wugu Sorcery in Imperial China: A Cross-Cultural Perspective," *Magic, Ritual, and Witchcraft* 8 (2013): 132–61.

38 Stoller and Olkes, *In Sorcery's Shadow*, 192.

39 Maarit Forde, "The Moral Economy of Spiritual Work: Money and Rituals in Trinidad and Tobago," in *Obeah and Other Powers: The Politics of Caribbean Religion and Healing*, eds. Diana Paton and Maarit Forde (Durham, NC: Duke University Press, 2012), 198–21.

40 Raquel Romberg, "The Moral Economy of Brujería under the Modern Colony: A Pirated Modernity?" in *Obeah and Other Powers*, 288–315; more fully in Raquel Romberg, *Witchcraft and Welfare: Spiritual Capital and the Business of Magic in Modern Puerto Rico* (Austin: University of Texas Press, 2003).

41 Raquel Romberg, *Healing Dramas: Divination and Magic in Modern Puerto Rico* (Austin: University of Texas Press, 2009), 14; Carol Ginzburg, *The Night Battles: Witchcraft and Agrarian Cults in the Sixteenth and Seventeenth Centuries*, trans. John and Anne Tedeschi (Baltimore, MD: Johns Hopkins University Press, 1983).

42 Lyndal Roper, *Oedipus and the Devil: Witchcraft, Sexuality and Religion in Early Modern Europe* (London: Routledge, 1994), is a good example of such work; also Lyndal Roper, *Witch Craze: Terror and Fantasy in Baroque Germany* (New Haven, CT: Yale University Press, 2004).

43 Helen Berger, *A Community of Witches: Contemporary Neo-Paganism and Witchcraft in the United States* (Columbia: University of South Carolina Press, 1999), xiii.

# 5

# THE REALITY OF MAGIC

Is magic real? The question is far from straightforward. Forget for a moment the problem of defining what magic is and focus instead on the problem of what "real" might mean. Have innumerable people, throughout history and down to the present day, believed that magic might help or harm them in very real ways? Yes. Have most human societies taken at least some kinds of magic quite seriously, either weaving magical rites into fundamental social practices or making certain forms of magic the target of strong reprobation and sometimes fearsome persecution? Absolutely. Are such people simply ignorant? Are such societies inherently backward and hopelessly befuddled about scientific principles of causation? The European anthropologists who inaugurated the modern academic study of magic in the late nineteenth and early twentieth centuries mostly concluded that believing in magic was a characteristic of primitive societies and primitive minds. As I outlined in Chapter 1, Edward Tylor, the founding father of academic anthropology in Britain in the late 1800s, thought about magic in patently evolutionary and racial terms. Belief in magic characterized "savage" races, while more advanced people developed sophisticated forms of religion and ultimately learned to put their faith in science. Such easy frameworks fall apart in many situations, however, and our understanding of magic has moved beyond them.

As I hope I have shown often enough already in this book, believing in magic is not just a characteristic of people living in premodern times. Nor is skepticism about magic confined to modern, enlightened minds. As argued in Chapter 3, the scope of magical power has long been a point of major contestation. Throughout history, serious, intelligent, and often highly educated people have asked themselves whether magic can cause changes in the physical world or the human mind. Some have answered yes, and some have answered no, although in fact, most have come down somewhere along a spectrum of belief (or skepticism), holding that some magical practices exert very real power and are worth either pursuing or persecuting with zealous fervor, while deeming other practices to be foolish and false. Tylor proclaimed magic to be "one of the most pernicious delusions that ever vexed mankind," but a tenth-century document from medieval Europe, the canon *Episcopi*, used equally judgmental language to castigate certain "wicked women" who believed that they traveled through the night with a spirit in the form of the pagan moon-goddess Diana, an image that would later inform the idea of witches flying to their unholy sabbaths during the era of Europe's major witch hunts. Yet, the canon (a document of church law) declared unequivocally that this idea was "in every way false," and it asked, "who is so stupid and foolish as to think that all these things which are only done in spirit happen in the body?"[1]

Now, there is certainly an important distinction to be drawn between these declarations by a modern anthropologist and a medieval text. Tylor was deriding all magic, or at least everything that he considered to be magical, whereas the canon *Episcopi* rejected only one belief associated with magic, namely that demons transported witches physically from place to place, to attend gatherings and work their harmful spells. The canon never doubted the reality of demons or their power. In fact, it was they, deceptive creatures that they were, who put the illusion of flight into the minds of muddle-headed women. But then, a Pew Research Center survey conducted in 2008 reported that two-thirds of Americans still believed that angels and demons remained active in some way in the modern world.[2]

This chapter will move past the aspect of magic's "reality" that rests on the simple fact that countless people have believed in it and many continue to do so. It will instead explore why they have believed. In doing so, however, it will also largely set aside the most elementary answer to that question; namely, that many people have accepted the reality of magic simply because the society in which they lived has asserted that it was real. No doubt that explanation is often apposite. People frequently believe that things they are told, by authorities they trust, must be true without giving the matter much more thought. But there has probably never been a society in which, however much the dominant intellectual, legal, or religious authorities may have proclaimed certain aspects of magic to be true, they have not also voiced skepticism about other kinds of magical practices, if not outright derision. Moreover, people also regularly doubt authority figures, refusing to accept what supposed experts advocate and refusing to abandon ideas that experts reject. This stubborn contrarianism is by no means a trait found only in our supposedly cynical modern age.

To better understand magic's reality beyond these basic parameters, in this chapter we will first examine ways in which magic might "really" work, producing at least some of the effects that it claims to, although not necessarily by the mechanisms that its practitioners assert. Then we'll explore reasons why people might choose to believe in magic even in the face of evident failures or despite powerful arguments made against magic's reality. This is a situation especially evident in the modern world, but not exclusively so. Finally, since belief is a matter of the mind, we'll look at how modern psychology has dealt with magic and whether there may be something inherent in the human brain that lends itself to believing in magic despite all our modern doubts.

## MAGIC THAT WORKS

Very often in the modern Western world, believing in the reality of magic is held up as the antithesis of clear-headed, rational, scientific thought. Physicist Robert Park, who wrote a book about modern superstitions, concluded his analysis with the powerful statement that "science is the only way of knowing." What he means, of course, is that he regards science as the only way of *truly* knowing anything about the world, while "everything else is just superstition."[3] Many people would dispute that claim, including other scientists and certainly many social scientists. Psychologist Eugene Subbotsky, who has written extensively about magical thinking, accepts that science is undoubtedly key to understanding the physical world we inhabit, but he notes, "the universe is much more than the physical: it includes [...] our mental and emotional lives, human relations and communication, fantasy, dreams, play, and art."[4] It is in these domains that he sees some value to magical modes of thought.

For Park, and even for Subbotsky, magical and scientific thinking involve very different ways of understanding cause and effect. As we have seen, however, throughout much of history the realm of magic has often mingled with what have been considered scientific forms of knowledge, and there is certainly some real science at the heart of certain magical practices. Many magical rites incorporate physical components such as herbs, minerals, and chemicals, for example, and these obviously have natural, scientifically under-standable properties. Utilizing such materials can be considered a form of "natural magic," a phrase that appears to have been coined by the thirteenth-century French scholastic William of Auvergne.[5] Of course, from the modern scientific perspective, the use of nat-ural properties is not magic at all. What would remain magical would be any extra ritual actions that people might perform while exploiting a natural substance or property; for example, reciting a charm or prayer while collecting medicinal herbs, or making certain ritualized gestures when administering a herbal remedy to a sick person. For the magician, these are important parts of the overall procedure, but for the scientist, they are ineffectual mumbo-jumbo. In either form of understanding, however, the procedure would have real effects.

We have already seen how, even in antiquity, the Roman natu-ralist Pliny the Elder was scathingly skeptical about many forms of natural magic (centuries before that term was coined), but he did not deny the wondrous properties of many natural substances. He reported, for example, that lotus berries were good for relieving diarrhea, while wood shavings boiled in wine were an excellent cure for dysentery, epilepsy, irregular menstruation, and vertigo. A poultice made from mistletoe was effective on wounds, tumors, and abscesses. Here Pliny also remarked, however, that some people "superstitiously believe" that this remedy could be made more ef-fective if the mistletoe was gathered under a new moon without the use of any iron implements and without letting it touch the ground after it had been picked. Like any modern scientist or physician, Pliny would never have labeled the medicinal uses of herbs, or other plants that he approved of and thought were naturally effective, as being magical. But his ideas of natural causation were somewhat different from those accepted by modern medicine. For example, he found that the root of the Polemonium plant (also known as Jacob's Ladder) was useful against scorpions, spiders, and other venomous animals, "even when merely attached to an amulet."[6] The Roman physician Dioscorides, who lived about the same time as Pliny, recorded similar wisdom in his *De materia medica* (On Medical Material), which remained a basic medical text in Europe until the sixteenth century.

In addition to plants, animal parts have often been thought to possess wondrous properties, especially medicinal ones. An appendix to a later medieval manuscript containing *De materia medica* offered several remedies concocted from the body parts of vultures. The bird's brains, for example, were presented as a good remedy for migraines when they were mixed with an unguent and snorted up the nose. Its testicles, when dried, pulverized, and mixed into wine, could cure impotence.[7] By no means would all such ancient and medieval recipes pass muster with modern science, but some of them would, at least in part. And in the past, the real efficacy of some procedures of this sort would certainly have added credence to that of other practices grouped around them.

As always with magic, where there is healing there can be harm. I have repeatedly noted how, throughout history, poisons of every sort have often been considered magical, and poisoners have been considered magicians. Poisoning was, for example, a common accusation at the root of many witch trials in early modern Europe.[8] The highly toxic plant atropa belladonna, also known as Deadly Nightshade, is just one noxious natural substance that has long been associated with witchcraft in the Western world. It has also been used, in controlled amounts, as an anesthetic in surgeries, and even as a cosmetic, to dilate women's pupils into what was considered a fetching, wide-eyed stare. Johan Wier, a sixteenth-century Dutch physician and great skeptic regarding most of the demonic aspects of witchcraft commonly accepted in his time, knew all about the power of plants like belladonna and hemlock, both as poisons and as hallucinogens, and attributed much of the reality of witches' magic to them.[9]

In addition to utilizing the natural properties of terrestrial plants, animals, and minerals, many magical systems from antiquity to the present have been built around the idea that heavenly bodies radiate specific energies toward the earth, and these rays can be harnessed and manipulated by those adept in such practices. Much has changed about our knowledge of the heavens over time, not least the discovery that the earth is itself a heavenly body revolving around the sun, rather than the center of the universe and the exclusive focus of all the other stars and planets. Most aspects of astral magic have lost what "scientific" credibility they once may have had as our understanding of cosmology has advanced. Nevertheless, it remains patently obvious that that sun radiates tremendous energy toward the earth, and the gravitational pull of the moon helps to create tides. The longstanding belief that a full moon will affect human behavior in various ways (from lunacy to lycanthropy) has repeatedly been debunked. Many studies have shown that emergency rooms are no busier on nights with a full moon than they are, on average, at any other time. Likewise, police records do not record more criminal activity at these times. In fact, periods of the full moon bear no correlation to increased crime, suicides, or psychiatric problems of any kind.[10] Nevertheless, even some trained emergency professionals act as if they do, preemptively adding staff to police precincts on nights of the full moon, for example.[11] And among the general populace, anyone who takes horoscopes seriously is at least unconsciously propounding the age-old notion that astral energies impart certain set characteristics to people at the moment of their birth.

Even ancient texts tend to differentiate astronomy, the science of observing or mathematically calculating the movement of the stars, from astrology, the practice of predicting human affairs based on those movements. The modern science of chemistry, on the other hand, only separated itself from premodern alchemy in the late-seventeenth and eighteenth centuries. Despite that direct and relatively recent connection, however, what could appear more fanciful to modern, scientific sensibilities than the image of an alchemist sweating before his furnace, laboring to transmute lead or some other base metal into gold? Even the basic physics through which such transmutations were once thought to be possible has been rejected. Western alchemy (we know of similar practices in India and China, but very little scholarship has focused on them) developed from ancient *chemeia* by way of medieval Arabic *al-kīmíyā'*. It operated mostly through controlled heating and cooling, meant to manipulate what Aristotle had declared were the four essential qualities of matter: heat, cold, moisture, and dryness. Nothing like a concept of chemical interaction at a molecular level is found in the intellectual apparatus of alchemy.

Nevertheless, the historian of science Lawrence Principe has found that, while alchemists' "theoretical explanations" for their processes were "flawed," many alchemical recipes do in fact produce results quite like what they purported. Since alchemists did not fully understand what they were doing, and since they tended to write in secretive and allegorical language, sometimes the success of an experiment can hinge on strict adherence to seemingly minor or tangential details. For example, one recipe attributed to the supposed German monk and alchemist Basil Valentine (probably a pseudonym for several alchemical writers whose works were later gathered together) purports to be able to purify poisonous qualities out of antimony sulfide, the ore known as stibnite. Valentine stressed using "Hungarian antinomy," and the experiment finally worked only when Principe obtained an ore sample from Eastern Europe. It turned out to contain an impurity. About two percent of its weight was quartz, and this allowed it to be "transformed" into the predicted glass-like form. Principe never found a recipe that would allow him to transform lead into gold, but he concluded that "the sight of remarkable and striking laboratory phenomenon," along with the fact that alchemy cohered with the best scientific principles of the day and was supported by ancient and respected authorities, made the elusive goal of the philosopher's stone seem a realistic one, certainly worth the pursuit.[12]

Another way in which magic "really" works is through deliberate and acknowledged artifice. While alchemists proved unable to create real gold, they were master counterfeiters and could certainly make other substances look like gold. That skill, too, could prove useful to princes or other wealthy clients, especially ones who wanted to seem wealthier than they were. Within the wider realm of magic, there has always been what we would now call stage magic, intended to entertain via deliberate trickery, of which the audience is usually well aware. Most people nowadays have probably seen such common stage illusions as a magician levitating an assistant or sawing a body in half. Another classic trick that remains in most modern stage magicians' repertoires is the cup-and-balls, in which a small ball (or dice, or another object) seemingly moves from one container to another. Such sleight-of-hand illusions are nothing new. The stoic philosopher Seneca the Younger, who died in 65 CE, refers in one of his "moral epistles" to the entertaining deception of "the juggler's cup and dice, in which it is the very trickery that pleases me."[13] Variants of this trick have been found in ancient India, China, and Japan, and other forms of entertaining illusions abounded. From tenth-century Iraq we have a text describing how a magician can fill a silk pouch with mercury, so people will think that it contains a slithering snake, and from fifteenth-century England we have a description of how to attach a slender human hair to a hollowed-out egg or small coin, so it can be made to move seemingly of its own accord.[14]

Beyond simple sleight-of-hand, magicians have sometimes deployed far more sophisticated mechanisms of trickery using mirrors, lenses, and other methods for producing optical illusions. This was particularly so in Europe during the Renaissance, when the science of optics was developing rapidly (somewhat in relation to another wonderful, albeit not magical, Renaissance optical development: the use of perspective in painting). The famous seventeenth-century Jesuit polymath Athanasius Kircher wrote what became the most sophisticated and famous account of optical magic, dedicating the final book of his *Ars magna lucis et umbrae* (Great Art of Light and Shadow) to the "Magic of Light and Shadow." One scholar credits him with creating what "might, at a stretch, qualify as Europe's first virtual reality device": a darkened room lit by a single window and fitted with a complex arrangement of mirrors that could produce a remarkable range of startling illusions.[15] Premodern magicians, although we might just as easily call them technicians, also created many kinds of automata to produce wonder and awe. The throne room of the Byzantine emperor in tenth-century Constantinople, for example, contained a tree made of gilded bronze with branches full of bronze birds that chirped and sang, and the throne itself was flanked by gilded bronze lions that could roar and thrash the floor with their tails.[16]

While most magic used for entertainment is based on the art of misdirection or mechanical trickery, other illusory experiences might stem from neurochemical effects. Among the many herbs and other natural substances associated with magic, quite a few have strong psychotropic properties, including some that can function as powerful hallucinogens. Those looking for some scientific basis for the more spectacular claims of magicians, and especially of witches and shamans, have often thought to find their answer in such drugs. This explanation-seeking is not new. I've already introduced the sixteenth-century skeptic Johan Wier, who argued that many claims made by accused witches about their allegedly demonic magical powers might be based instead in mental delusions. Sometimes this could occur because of simple melancholy, an imbalance of humors that affected the mind of the supposed witch (what we'd now consider mental illness), but sometimes, he argued, mind-altering drugs could also be involved. He recounted various "witches' unguents" containing such highly toxic substances as belladonna, hemlock, aconite, and henbane. Wier quoted accounts by other early modern authorities about how witches would use these ointments, smearing them on their bodies and then experiencing sensations of imagined flight to demonic sabbaths.[17]

Such explanations appeal to modern, scientific sensibilities, but we need to treat them with considerable caution. Careful research now suggests that the specific ointments cataloged in historical texts might be as much figments of early demonologists' imaginations as the witches' sabbath itself. While many early modern authorities writing about witchcraft described these ointments and their use, accused witches almost never did, unless during a trial they were compelled to do so by their judges, usually under the threat or application of torture. Modern experts, this new research argues, have been too quick to accept the reality of such ointments, precisely because they seem to provide a scientific, chemical explanation for some of the gross delusions that fueled Europe's major witch hunts.[18] Likewise, we should be skeptical of the suggestion that certain major outbreaks of witch-hunting, most famously that at Salem, Massachusetts, in 1692, could be connected to ergotism, a disease caused by eating grain contaminated with ergot fungus and manifesting as convulsions and delirium that could be taken as signs of bewitchment or demonic possession. Descriptions of afflicted people in witchcraft cases only resemble ergotism very loosely, and we obviously have no way to test grain supplies from centuries ago. In any event, when ergotism occurs, it usually infects an entire grain supply and affects an entire community, not a few targeted victims, such as the handful of seemingly bewitched young girls at Salem.

Despite the caution necessary in these cases, it remains clear that magicians the world over have indeed made use of hallucinogenic substances. In addition, mystics and shamans throughout history have demonstrated other means that can be used to induce altered or trance-like states, from rhythmic music and dancing to silent meditation. Generally, such practitioners know that the experiences they have while in an altered state are only mental or spiritual, but in many cultures such experiences are regarded as being just as "real" and significant as physical reality, if not more so.

An enormous amount of magic may, in fact, take place in the mind, not though such complex mechanisms as pharmacology or altered states, but simply through the natural operation of suggestion and perception. Medical science is aware of the placebo effect. If patients think that they are receiving treatment even when they are not, often their condition will improve nonetheless. Healing charms, amulets, and herbal remedies (even leaving aside the fact that they might have some chemical or nutrient benefit) would work in similar ways. Conversely, real harm can also be done solely by the power of suggestion. To those who believe in the power of magic, just the suspicion that a witch may have cast a harmful spell on them can induce serious anxiety and real physical stress. This would be exacerbated if a person then discovered some horrible evidence of witchcraft, such as a magical totem buried under the threshold of his or her house, or perhaps a conjure bag from the African-American tradition stuffed with hair, nails, or animals' bones and placed near an intended victim. And of course, there is always the possibility of a stressful encounter with the witch herself, in which she might spitefully curse the person to his or her face.

Under the right conditions, fear can be instilled even in a skeptic. An anthropologist studying witchcraft in Indonesia who felt himself very much an adherent of modern rationalism nevertheless recounted how disturbed he became when, one night, he heard sounds like a dog chewing a bone. But these sounds seemed to come from the roof of his house, which was patently impossible because the house had a leaf roof, and even if a dog had managed to clamber up, it would have instantly fallen through. After some tense moments lying in bed, he finally grabbed a flashlight and went outside to look, but he found nothing. The sound went away, but the experience remained unsettlingly "eerie."[19]

In this part of Indonesia, the evil spirit of a witch, *gua*, can take many forms, but often it is thought to flit around at night somewhat like a bat. Imagine the stress, then, that would be produced in a pregnant woman waking up to find what she took to be a *gua* crouching on her stomach. One such woman, whose case was recorded, developed a severe fever the very next day, although ultimately, she recovered without any permanent harm.[20] *Gua* also frequently take the form of birds, and sudden or especially shrill calls deemed to come from such "witch-birds" can induce feelings of panic in whole households or even entire neighborhoods. Traditionally people would counter these malevolent calls with their own vocalizations in the form of chanted counter-spells, but now in modern Indonesia they can also employ technology, playing TVs or CDs loudly, not just as entertainment but to block out any baleful witch-sounds that might come from the treetops.[21]

In many places, witches not only manifest as animals, striking fear into the humans who see or hear them, but they also count animals among their victims. Some scholars suggest even this may be a mental process, with domestic animals picking up on their owners' anxieties. Thus a peasant who thinks his cows have been bewitched might himself be the agent of this bewitchment, in the sense that he believes himself to be the target of witchcraft, he becomes anxious about this, his animals sense his anxiety, and they become anxious too, causing them either to sicken, to give less milk, or to reproduce less successfully.[22] It probably need not be said how anxiety and stress might affect human reproductive behavior, and how this could relate to countless stories of men bewitched into impotency or women induced to miscarry.

Another very real dynamic is that, aside from possibly inducing physiological changes through stress, the suspicion that magical forces are in play may cause people to perceive reality differently, seeing occult causality where otherwise they might only find coincidence, or even seeing things that simply are not there. Of course, all sensory perception is ultimately indirect. We do not actually see the light waves that our eyes take in. Rather, our brains interpret the sensory signals that our eyes send out. Quite literally, we see what we think we see. And if conditioned properly, sometimes we can see remarkable things indeed. In 1692, just as the major Salem witch hunt was beginning to gear up in Massachusetts, in the neighboring colony of Connecticut, a group of people from the town of Stamford gathered at the home of Daniel Wescot to observe the strange fits and convulsions that had suddenly begun to afflict his maidservant, Katherine Branch, who some said was bewitched. Leaving aside what Kate may have been feeling, or feigning, and why, some of her observers experienced remarkable events. One felt a stabbing pain in his side. Kate helpfully confirmed that it was an invisible witch pricking him. Another saw a "ball of fire as big as my two hands" move across the room and disappear into the hearth. Another saw Kate's breasts swell like two bladders and then collapse again against her chest. Yet, another saw her tongue roll out of her mouth to an enormous length, and then, when it retracted and he peered into her mouth, he saw only a lump of raw meat.[23]

What is remarkable here is that this community, while obviously believing in the possibility of witchcraft, was not yet firmly convinced that witchcraft was at play in this case. Many in Stamford thought Kate was dissembling, and the purpose of observing her was to see if she was afflicted or not. Ultimately, a couple of trials were conducted, but only one resulted in a conviction, which was soon overturned. Unlike Salem, Stamford was not characterized by unbridled panic. And yet some sober members of the community claimed they saw or felt clear signs of witchcraft. Possibly they were lying, but since the presence of witchcraft was not yet that widely accepted, they would have had no reason to make up spectacular tales just to jump on some bandwagon. More likely, given the situation in which they found themselves and the stresses and tensions it induced, they really saw what they said they did.

## LEARNING TO BELIEVE

Abraham Finch, the stalwart Puritan who saw the ball of fire move across Katherine Branch's bedchamber, was deeply shaken by the sight. When other witnesses arrived, they found him deathly pale. But why did he believe that what he had seen was real? The analysis I've offered so far would posit that he found himself in a very stressful situation, alone in a dark room, watching over a young woman said (by some) to be afflicted by witchcraft. He was presumably tense and jittery, and under the pressure of the moment, he really did see a fiery orb pass before him. He would have been ready to ascribe this to witchcraft because, obviously, he lived in a society that accepted the reality of such things.

But remember that many residents of Stamford did not, in fact, believe that Kate Branch had been bewitched. They may have accepted the possibility that malevolent witches were active somewhere in the world, but they did not think that such power was present in this case, and they suspected instead that Kate was just a dissembling young woman looking for attention. Regarding poor Abraham, these skeptics must have thought either that he was lying, too, or that he was a bit looney. It is also important to note that levitating fireballs were not a typical manifestation of witchcraft in colonial New England. Conditioned as we now are by movies and television, we often think of magic in terms of lightning bolts and glowing orbs. In fact, most forms of magic are far more mundane, and far less visually spectacular. A sick person either gets well or grows sicker. A relationship, amorous or otherwise, intensifies or goes sour. Someone either does or does not complete a successful journey. A thunderstorm either damages crops or it abates and leaves them largely unscathed. Such events are not self-evidently magical. Instead, people learn to interpret them in particular ways.

Even in societies that broadly believe in the power of magic, people know that sometimes the healthy get sick and the sick recover for entirely natural reasons; that in some years the harvest will be bountiful while in others it will be marred by storms, drought or vermin; and that all too often the person you absolutely adore is going to ignore you in favor of some complete goon without any malevolent spell or love potion being to blame. Belief in magic is not just about a society deeming magic to be real or not, but also about individuals within that society deciding whether they believe that this or that discrete event has been caused by magic, even though other explanations are readily available. A great deal of anthropological and historical scholarship has endeavored to uncover what social or cultural factors might contribute to the belief that magic is in operation in particular instances. Since our largest body of evidence in this regard comes from witchcraft trials and accusations, let's begin there.

Anthropologists have long favored, and historians have largely accepted, the idea that witchcraft accusations function, in part, as a gauge for underlying social tensions. Here's a generic example. Someone close to you gets sick. You think nothing of it. You know that occasional bouts of illness are perfectly normal and natural. But if a loved one gets sick just after you have had a run-in with the sour old woman who lives down the road and who spat curses at you as she stormed off, then you might think very differently indeed. Or maybe you've recently had an altercation with a neighbor. He expressed sharp animosity toward you, and you returned the feeling in spades. No overt threats were made, but the next time you or someone in your household gets sick or has an accident, you'll remember the incident and wonder whether nefarious magic might be at work. Your neighbor could have cast a spell himself or maybe he went to that old women down the road. In any event, you are convinced that someone is directing malevolent forces at you and yours.

Or maybe you worry that your own actions are attracting such forces. Another general social explanation for witchcraft is that it functions as a form of social control. We've already seen how people identified as witches are frequently social outsiders of some kind. But this explanation can also bear on self-perceived victims of magical assault. Studies of witchcraft from early modern Europe to modern Southeast Asia suggest that people are more inclined to suspect that they are targets of malevolent witchcraft if they feel that they themselves have recently transgressed some social norm. Perhaps they have acted uncharitably toward friends or neighbors, ignored a family member in need or shirked some important social obligation.

In the small community of Buli in eastern Indonesia, when someone returns from hunting to fishing, a crowd will inevitably gather. In part, these people lend assistance, carrying heavy gear or pulling a canoe securely onto the beach. They will also typically comment about the bounty of the catch. It is then incumbent on the successful fisherman or hunter to offer some of this bounty to the expectant crowd. Understandably, a man who has just spent many hours of strenuous effort fishing at sea or hunting in the jungle might be somewhat resentful of the generosity he's now expected to show. But any excessive "grumbling" at the obligation is regarded as a moral failing that can render one vulnerable to witchcraft.[24]

Likewise, in early modern England, suspicions of witchcraft were often tied to some breach of social etiquette, most often a breach of charity toward a neighbor. In this scenario, maybe that sour but ultimately poor and helpless old woman from down the road cursed at you because you refused her a bit of butter when she came begging at your door. Normally you're not the sort to attribute your troubles to witchcraft, but if anything should go seriously amiss in your household now, you will feel certain that you know why. Some historical scholarship has even suggested that the overall surge of witch trials in Europe in the sixteenth and seventeenth centuries might be connected to this dynamic. Greater numbers of accusations were, in this analysis, driven by rising tensions as increasingly individualistic early modern society gradually but unevenly supplanted the communal charity patterns of the earlier medieval period.[25] This argument has been subjected to much criticism, as any sweeping theory is bound to be, but the basic proposition that people are more willing to suspect magic as the cause of misfortune during moments of marked social tension certainly holds up.

Another basic proposition is that people are more apt to believe in magical malevolence during extended periods of hardship or crisis. Historians have long noted that the peak of witch-hunting during the sixteenth and seventeenth centuries coincided with Europe's so-called "iron century" (1550–1650), when much of the continent was wracked by religious reformations and bloody religious wars, major economic and social change, and a "little ice age" of general climactic cooling that affected crop production and made life more difficult for millions of people. Modern parallels are not hard to find. Widespread belief in witches in Africa stems from many factors, but the devastating explosion of AIDS across much of the continent since the 1990s has played a major role.[26]

Again, however, any sweeping explanation will have its limits. Witch-hunting did not break out on any significant scale, for example, when Europe underwent its greatest biological catastrophe: the onset of the Black Death in the middle of the fourteenth century. Some rumors about Jews poisoning wells circulated at this time, but in general people seem to have attributed the tremendous devastation all around them to an angry God – or to unfavorable astral conditions, as the medical faculty of the University of Paris determined in a ruling it issued in 1348.[27]

While we must always remain cautious of singular, grand theories that purport to explain complex social behaviors, it certainly appears true across history and cultures that people frequently become ready to believe in magic during hard times and in the face of severe problems, especially when other means to explain or remedy those problems are unavailable or appear to have failed. Not only are people more likely to suspect the presence of witchcraft under such circumstances, but they are also more inclined to turn to magic themselves, either performing simple rites directly or seeking out professional practitioners who offer to help them in their need. This argument can easily loop back into the position that magic is endemic in "primitive" societies that lack proper scientific explanations and remedies for misfortune, so it is worth stressing again that no premodern societies have ever believed in magic as the sole cause of all misfortune. Nor do people in these societies necessarily expect magic to provide reliable remedies or afford them complete control over life's many vicissitudes. They understand that sometimes children will still get sick, harvests will fail, and economic ventures will collapse even if all possible magical precautions are taken. It is, in fact, science, not magic, that holds out the hope of complete control over nature and the (eventual) technological solution to all problems.

Thus, it is not uncertainty or lack of control, per se, that fosters belief in magic, but excessive uncertainty or some particularly disconcerting lack of control. This remains just as true in the modern world as in premodern and pre-scientific societies. Consider the situation in present-day Africa, where belief in witchcraft remains widespread across much of the continent, but where people are also fully exposed to the modern (Western) mindset that magic is not real. Many want to accept that modern position, but unsurprisingly they find it easier to do so when most of the basic conditions in their lives are good and more difficult to do so in times of exceptional difficulty or stress.[28] Or consider psychological studies that focus on people under extraordinary stress. One such study compared Israeli citizens living in areas prone to missile attack to those living in safe zones during the first Gulf War (1990–1991). As would only be expected, those who lived in areas subject to frequent missile attack were considerably more likely to exhibit "magical thinking" than those in safer, more stable areas. That is, they acted as if magical rites or superstitious actions might have real effects, whether or not they professed to believe in such magic. In fact, many continued to express the accepted modern stance that magic is not real even as they engaged in superstitious rites or otherwise acted as if such rites might be effective.[29]

So far, I have been discussing social, cultural, and some psychological factors that may increase the likelihood that people will suspect magical forces to be in operation, turn to magic themselves, and at least act as if they believe magic is real. These factors are surprisingly similar across premodern and modern societies, and between those cultures that broadly believe in magic and the culture of Western modernity that largely does not. Of course, it will always be easier for an individual to express belief in magic in a society that is accepting of that belief. But how exactly does an entire society come to believe?

Often the answer to that question simply resurrects the "primitivism" argument yet again. That is, belief in magic is posited to be a basic condition of pre-scientific societies and peoples. All that needs explaining, historically, is how one society, the modern West, moved to a condition of widespread disbelief in magic. But here is where studies of magical believers in modern Western society can offer an interesting and illuminating perspective. The anthropologist T. M. Luhrmann conducted extensive research among modern Witches and ritual magicians living in England at the end of the twentieth century. She found these magical practitioners to be well-educated and middle-class. Moreover, they usually started from a position of significant skepticism about the possibility of real magical operations. Often their forays into magic began more as a hobby or recreation than a serious pursuit. But then, "by some process, when they get involved in magic...they learn to find it eminently sensible."[30]

I want to focus here on three significant insights that emerge from Luhrmann's efforts to explain that process. First, practicing magic can, over time, alter how people perceive and interpret events. Through the very rituals they perform, and by discussing how such magical rites operate, practitioners condition themselves (Luhrmann describes the process as "learning") to see meaningful patterns in what others would take to be random events and to discern connections and causality where others would see only co-incidence. One could, of course, simply say that they are fooling themselves, but if that is the case, they are doing so in a very sophisticated way. Scholars have always recognized that believing in magic involves seeing different kinds of cause and effect relationships than modern science will allow. Luhrmann's insight is to show how this mindset does not exist statically or erupt from some primitive recess of our brains, but is in fact actively developed by the performance of magic itself.

Luhrmann's second insight is that magicians are comfortable seeing the effects of their magic as being either direct or indirect. That is, in some circumstances, they perceive that a magical rite has accomplished the exact, concrete thing it was intended to do. But in other circumstances, they readily adopt a position in which they maintain that the rite may not have resulted in any concrete effect but nevertheless had psychological, spiritual or expressive value for them personally. As she notes, practitioners frequently assert the "value" of believing in magic, rather than its "truth," and they often move easily back and forth between these positions.[31] Nevertheless, in what I see as her third important insight, Luhrmann also argues that, however "loose" the criteria for judging magic's success can sometimes become, they must remain strict enough that there is always a possibility of clear, unambiguous failure. Far from being a blow to their belief, experiencing magical rites that fail critically reinforces the magicians' conviction that they are engaging in a serious activity that operates in an objective and not merely an imagined way.

We can see throughout history that persistent failures have never undermined most practitioners' basic beliefs. The worried parent who performs a healing spell over her sick child but then watches its fever grow worse will not lose faith in magic but simply conclude that, in this instance, the disease was too strong for the magic to overcome. The alchemist disappointed for the umpteenth time at finding only ordinary lead in his furnace will conclude that he has yet to discover the exact proportions necessary to effect a transmutation.

Although the fact that Luhrmann studied modern magicians operating in a society that is broadly skeptical about magic shaped her research in fundamental ways, I think that her other insights can be applied to premodern societies as well. Particularly, they can help show us how people living in societies that accept the reality of various forms of magic are not simply mired in primordial ignorance. Rather, the magic that they and their neighbors perform directly, as well as that which they see or are told is performed by recognized magical experts, continually "teaches" these people how to believe in magic and how to perceive its operations as effective and real.

## MAGIC AND THE BRAIN

Humanity's continued belief in magic has fascinated modern psychology for almost as long as it has modern anthropology. Both Freud and especially Jung were interested in various kinds of magic, although their work in this area is no longer so influential as some early anthropological theories of magic remain (I'll discuss them more fully in Chapter 6). In fact, many psychologists continue to regard magic in ways similar to early anthropologists. They see magical or superstitious thinking as evidence of an underdeveloped mental state. Rather than "primitive," they describe serious belief in the power of magic as being a characteristic of childhood thought, perhaps even a natural state into which we are born, but one which, if we are so lucky as to live in properly developed societies, we should outgrow as we age and become educated. They are certainly not wrong about the ingrained nature of magical thinking, in that many aspects of magic appear to stem from or at least mesh well with some basic components of human cognition. Certain factors that contribute to belief in magic may even lie deep in our evolution.

To being, let's look at a couple of basic frameworks for magic identified by early anthropological studies and see how they reflect psychological characteristics. In his classic work *The Golden Bough*, James Frazer argued that primitive people frequently thought about magic as operating by means of a "secret sympathy," which manifested either through similarity or contagion.[32] In magic that operates through similarity, things that resemble one another in some way are thought to influence or control each other. Simple examples include stirring water in a bucket to conjure a rainstorm, or crafting an image made to resemble a certain person and then inflicting harm on the figure to injure that person. In contagious magic, things that have once been in contact are thought to continue affecting each other at a distance. A spell might use a piece of a person's clothing, a lock of hair or a drop of blood to exploit the magical connection.

Both these kinds of practice represent symbolic and ritual elaborations grounded in some basic psychological factors. We are, it appears, naturally predisposed to assume deeper connections between things that in some way resemble one another. For example, in experiments, people who have no trouble holding a small bit of rubber in their mouths for a few seconds prove to be much more reluctant to do so when the rubber resembles feces. Many people are also reluctant to drink what they know to be pure water from a bottle labeled "cyanide," even if they themselves are the ones who have labeled and filled the bottle. These are not pointless characteristics. It is obviously advantageous, when in doubt, to avoid unknown food, plants or other substances that in some way resemble known harmful substances. Likewise, it is safest to assume that things that have been in contact with dangerous substances may have picked up some harmful quality themselves.[33]

Belief in magic also appears to be facilitated by the way our memory works. Humans tend to remember moments of success better than moments of failure. Modern magicians certainly tend to fix in their memories those occasions on which their rites appear to have been effective, while they brush aside instances that offer little or no clear signs of magical effects.[34] Conversely, human beings also tend to remember "if only" scenarios quite vividly; that is, we powerfully recall negative outcomes that we imagine could have been altered by some action we failed to take. Thus, the magician will remember the time she didn't use a magical rite and lost a competition, failed to get a job, or so forth, rather than those occasions on which she either used a rite and it had no effect or did not use a rite and still had a successful outcome.[35]

Magical practices are often thought to answer our psychological need to feel that we have some basic control over events in our lives and to impose a certain order onto the unknown. A very standard argument is that magical beliefs are more prevalent in premodern societies than modern ones because science and technology have now given us objectively better ways to understand and control the world around us. And in the modern world, the same argument runs, magic remains more prevalent in less developed and less wealthy societies because they have less access to the full range of modern scientific and technological resources. Furthermore, even in wealthy Western societies, superstitious thinking, if not necessarily magic per se, appears to have remained more prevalent among people whose professions or pastimes involve higher levels of randomness or risk than is common in the rest of society. Studies suggest that soldiers and sailors, but also gamblers and actors, hold such beliefs at higher rates than other groups.[36] I have already discussed how common it can be for people to turn to magic in moments of severe stress, when it may seem to them that they have lost whatever level of control they usually have over their lives, and this argument is partly an extension of that basic point.

While this general approach to understanding magic makes a great deal of sense, it can also be pushed too far or applied too simplistically. While some psychological studies have tried to show that higher levels of education specifically in science and engineering correlate with a lower proclivity for superstitious and magical thinking, other studies indicate no correlation at all. Moreover, many studies have shown that levels of belief in magic or superstitions have remained remarkably constant within Western societies since at least the very early twentieth century when such surveys began to be taken. Steadily advancing science and technology, therefore, does not lead to any directly parallel or proportional decline in magical beliefs.

Indeed, historically Western European society did not gradually abandon magical practices piecemeal as science, technology or medicine became advanced enough to provide more reliable solutions to everyday problems. Instead, mainly during the period of the eighteenth-century Enlightenment, intellectual elites in Western Europe largely abandoned their belief in magic altogether, and then worked to impose their new rationality on the rest of Western society. Where only a few decades earlier courts had burned witches, for example, they now prosecuted people claiming to practice magic for committing fraud.

There is also an obvious counter-point to the argument that magic serves to alleviate uncertainty and provide some measure of control; namely, that magical practices themselves are often ambiguous, uncertain, and uncontrollable. There is a psychological principle at work here as well. As much as people enjoy feeling safe and secure, they do not always seek out absolute certainty and predictability. That would be boring, and part of our psychological makeup is attuned to enjoy some level of randomness and chance.[37] Magic can fill this need, too, and so people turn to it for entertainment, amusement, and thrill-seeking, as well as to redress problems and reduce uncertainty.

Given that magic itself can be extremely fluid and variable, we shouldn't expect people to have altogether clear and fixed attitudes or motivations regarding it. In fact, psychological studies have found that belief in magic is often a classic example of dual-process thinking. That is, many people who consciously and intentionally disbelieve that magical rites can produce real physical effects may still behave as if they do believe. This is not a matter of going along with some magical belief because it is entertaining or fun or because it is psychologically easier in certain situations. Careful experimentation suggests that people do, at some level, believe, even though they absolutely and truthfully profess that they do not.

One well-known phenomenon along these lines is the reluctance many people exhibit to exchange one lottery ticket for another before a drawing. In fact, many people will refuse to give up "their" ticket even if they are offered a small incentive to do so. These people fully understand that all tickets have an equal chance of winning. Typically, they explain that they would be particularly disappointed if the ticket they gave away ended up being the winning one, more so than whatever the incentive offered for making the exchange is worth to them. This is called regret avoidance, and it is a recognized psychological principle. Through various kinds of testing, however, some psychologists have found that many people behave as if the act of giving away "their" ticket will increase the odds of it being a winner. They are not lying when they profess to understand (and to believe) that all tickets have an equal chance of winning. Yet, at some powerful level, they equally believe that their actions might affect those odds.[38]

Studies by developmental psychologists have shown that children growing up in modern Western societies learn to express disbelief in magic long before they come to reject magical beliefs themselves. Extrapolating from this, the psychologist Eugene Subbotsky argues that even in adults, belief in magic is only "repressed" and can be "reactivated" in various ways.[39] The basic conclusion here would again be that belief in magic is somehow innate to us, and we must learn to overcome it, although we can never do so completely. I would suggest that this conclusion must be combined somehow with the insight that belief in magic can also be a learned characteristic.

Although modern psychological studies focus, self-evidently, on modern people, there can be little doubt that people throughout history have also behaved, in accordance with dual-process thinking, as if they were of two minds about magic. In Chapter 2, we saw how the seventeenth-century Chinese intellectual Wang Bu derided magical spells, but then used one himself when he feared that he was confronted by a demon. Likewise, the versatile Roman author Pliny the Elder derided superstitious beliefs and recommended that other educated people should do so as well. Nevertheless, he also noted how there was "no one" who was not at least somewhat afraid of being bound by evil spells or who would refuse to perform ritual actions to ward off the threat of the evil eye.[40]

One imagines Pliny's attitude being not unlike that expressed in the famous quip attributed to the twentieth-century physicist Niels Bohr. A friend supposedly noted that Bohr had a horseshoe affixed above his door and asked incredulously whether the great scientist believed in such superstitions. "Of course not," Bohr is supposed to have replied, "but I understand it's lucky whether you believe in it or not."[41] If the Nobel Prize winner ever said something like this, he was far from alone. His remark finds echoes across the modern word, for example in the waiting room of a Puerto Rican *bruja*, a witch-healer, where a scholar once heard a client declare, "I don't believe in brujería, but it works."[42]

There are certainly some eminently practical, one might even say hard-nosed, modern professionals who are perfectly aware of how certain rituals and verbal formulas can alter our beliefs, if not reality itself: advertising executives and political advisers. In the 1930s, the anthropologist Bronislaw Malinowski recognized the basic similarity between magical rites used by the Trobriand Islanders he was studying in the South Pacific and modern advertising and political rhetoric, and other scholars have reinforced the connection since then.[43] Both advertising and political rhetoric intend to make us desire certain things, reject others, and adopt stances that we previously did not hold. At their most powerful, they compel us to change our attitudes, perhaps even our beliefs, without our being aware that they are doing so. In similar ways, magical rites may actively foster belief in people who were previously skeptical or who profess to remain so.

One final psychological characteristic needs to be discussed, which I will also connect to the suggestion that engaging in magical practices may teach people how to believe in them. Certain people, we know, are more receptive to powerful imaginative and perceptual experiences than others. In psychological terms, this is called "high absorption." It is, for example, a factor in why some people respond to music or art more strongly than others, become lost in films or fiction more easily or just daydream more readily. Most psychologists regard it as a fixed mental characteristic. The anthropologist Tanya Luhrmann, however, whom we have already met through her studies of modern magicians, argues that people can learn to become more highly absorptive through certain ritual behaviors. In this case, her study focuses on Evangelical Christian prayer practices and how they serve to teach these people to hear what they perceive as the voice of God, but she draws connections to her earlier work on magical rituals as well.[44] It has long been known that shamans and mystics sometimes perform elaborate rituals to prepare themselves for intense sensory and spiritual experiences. Luhrmann suggests that equally earnest but less extravagant practices can also shape how we perceive, and hence what we believe, in profound ways.

So, is magic real? It may not operate the way practitioners claim that it does, but then again, ambiguity and uncertainty are central features in most kinds of magical practice anyway, and practitioners are rarely concerned with understanding exactly how their magic works. Magical practices, or practices that have in many contexts been considered to be magical, can produce physical effects in manifold ways, and magical beliefs resonate with some basic aspects of human psychology. Most intriguing of all is how magical practices themselves may guide practitioners toward greater levels of belief. It seems fair to end this chapter by confessing that I myself am of two minds. I remain among those who do not believe in magic, but I am far from willing to assert that it is not real.

## NOTES

1 Alan Charles Kors and Edward Peters, eds., *Witchcraft in Europe 400–1700: A Documentary History*, 2nd ed. (Philadelphia: University of Pennsylvania Press, 2001), 62.

2 Cited in Tanya M. Luhrmann, *When God Talks Back: Understanding the American Evangelical Relationship with God* (New York: Vintage, 2012), xi.

3 Robert L. Park, *Superstition: Belief in the Age of Science* (Princeton, NJ: Princeton University Press, 2008), 215.

4 Eugene Subbotsky, *Magic and the Mind: Mechanisms, Functions, and Development of Magical Thinking and Behavior* (Oxford: Oxford University Press, 2010), x.

5 Jean-Patrice Boudet, *Entre science et nigromance: Astrologie, divination et magie dans l'Occident médiéval (XIIe-XVe siècle)* (Paris: Sorbonne, 2006), 128.

6 Pliny, *Natural History* 24.2, 24.6, 25.72, trans. William Henry Samuel Jones, vol. 7 (Cambridge, MA: Harvard University Press, 1956).

7 Richard Kieckhefer, *Magic in the Middle Ages* (Cambridge: Cambridge University Press, 1989), 66.

8 Edward Bever, *The Realities of Witchcraft and Popular Magic in Early Modern Europe: Culture, Cognition, and Everyday Life* (New York: Palgrave Macmillan, 2008), 8.

9 Wier, *De praestigiis daemonum* 3.17; see *On Witchcraft: An Abridged Translation of Johann Weyer's De praestigiis daemonum*, ed. Benjamin G. Kohl and H. C. Erik Midelfort (Ashville, NC: Pegasus, 1998), 114–16.

10 James Rotton and Ivan W. Kelly, "Much Ado about the Full Moon: A Meta-analysis of Lunar-Lunacy Research," *Psychological Bulletin* 97, no. 2 (March 1985): 286–306.

11 Scott O. Lilienfeld and Hall Arkowitz, "Lunacy and the Full Moon," *Scientific American Mind* 20, no. 1 (Feb/March 2009): 64–65.

12 Lawrence M. Principe, *The Secrets of Alchemy* (Chicago, IL: University of Chicago Press, 2013), 137–71, quotes at 143, 170.

13 Epistle 45, in Lucius Annaeus Seneca, *Moral Epistles*, trans. Richard M. Gummere, 3 vols. (Cambridge, MA: Harvard University Press, 1917–1925).

14 Owen Davies, *Magic: A Very Short Introduction* (Oxford: Oxford University Press, 2012), 51; Kieckhefer, *Magic in the Middle Ages*, 91.

15 Stuart Clark, *Vanities of the Eye: Vision in Early Modern European Culture* (Oxford: Oxford University Press, 2007), 99–104, quote at 103.

16 Kieckhefer, *Magic in the Middle Ages*, 101.

17 Wier, *De praestigiis daemonum* 3.17.

18 Michael Ostling, "Babyfat and Belladonna: Witches' Ointment and the Contestation of Reality," *Magic, Ritual, and Witchcraft* 11 (2016): 30–72.

19 Nils Bubandt, *The Empty Seashell: Witchcraft and Doubt on an Indonesian Island* (Ithaca, NY: Cornell University Press, 2014), ix–x.

20 Bubandt, *Empty Seashell*, 127–28.

21 Bubandt, *Empty Seashell*, 218–20.

22 Bever, *Realities of Witchcraft*, 37–38.

23 Richard Godbeer, *Escaping Salem: The Other Witch Hunt of 1692* (Oxford: Oxford University Press, 2005), 26–32.

24 Bubandt, *Empty Seashell*, 199–200.

25 An argument associated with Alan Macfarlane, *Witchcraft in Tudor and Stuart England: A Regional and Comparative Study* (London: Routledge, 1970); and chiefly with Keith Thomas, *Religion and the Decline of Magic* (New York: Scribner's, 1971).

26 Adam Ashforth, *Witchcraft, Violence, and Democracy in South Africa* (Chicago, IL: University of Chicago Press, 2005), 105–10.

27 Rosemary Horrox, ed. and trans., *The Black Death* (Manchester: Manchester University Press, 1994), 158–63.

28 Ashforth, *Witchcraft, Violence, and Democracy*, 123.

29 Giora Keinan, "Effects of Stress and Tolerance of Ambiguity on Magical Thinking," *Journal of Personality and Social Psychology* 67 (1994): 48–55.

30 Tanya M. Luhrmann, *Persuasions of the Witch's Craft: Ritual Magic in Contemporary England* (Cambridge, MA: Harvard University Press, 1989), 7.

31 Luhrmann, *Persuasions*, 283, 333.

32 James George Frazer, *The Golden Bough: A Study of Religion and Magic*, new abridgement, ed. Robert Fraser (Oxford: Oxford University Press, 1994), 26–27.

33 Paul Rozin and Carol Nemeroff, "Sympathetic Magical Thinking: The Contagion and Similarity 'Heuristics,'" in *Heuristics and Biases: The Psychology of Intuitive Judgment*, ed. Thomas Gilovich, Dale Griffin, and Daniel Kahneman (Cambridge: Cambridge University Press, 2002), 201–16.

34 Luhrmann, *Persuasions*, 125.

35 Dale T. Miller and Brian R. Taylor, "Counterfactual Thought, Regret, and Superstition: How to Avoid Kicking Yourself," in *Heuristics and Biases*, 367–78.

36 Leonard Zusne and Warren H. Jones, *Anomalistic Psychology: A Study of Magical Thinking*, 2nd ed. (Hillsdale, NJ: Lawrence Erlbaum Associates, 1989), 15.

37 Gustav Jahoda, *The Psychology of Superstition* (London: Allen Lane, 1969), 134–35.

38 Jane L. Risen and Thomas Gilovich, "Another Look at Why People are Reluctant to Exchange Lottery Tickets," *Journal of Personality and Social Psychology* 93 (2007): 12–22.

39 Subbotsky, *Magic and the Mind*, 51.

40 Pliny, *Natural History*, 28.4, 28.5.

41 The earliest record of this anecdote appears to be in E. E. Kenyon, "The Wit Parade," *American Weekly* section of *The Cleveland Plain*

*Dealer*, Sept. 30, 1956, p. 13; as determined by http://quoteinvestigator.
com/2013/10/09/horseshoe-luck/ (accessed February 7, 2017).

42 Raquel Romberg, *Witchcraft and Welfare: Spiritual Capital and the Business of Magic in Modern Puerto Rico* (Austin: University of Texas Press, 2003), 3.

43 Bronislaw Malinowski, *Coral Gardens and Their Magic, Volume 2: The Language of Magic and Gardening* (1935; reprint Bloomington: Indiana University Press, 1965), 237–38; see also Peter Geschiere, "On Witch Doctors and Spin Doctors: The Role of 'Experts' in African and American Politics," in *Magic and Modernity: Interfaces of Revelation and Concealment*, ed. Birgit Meyer and Peter Pels (Stanford, CA: Stanford University Press, 2003), 159–82; Subbotsky, *Magic and the Mind*, 96–114. Both Geschiere and Subbotsky credit Malinowski's insight.

44 Luhrmann, *When God Talks Back*, 190–92, 202.

# 6

# MAGIC IN THE MODERN WORLD

The French philosopher Michel Foucault once quipped that, although much of his work dealt with the history of ideas, he was not a professional historian, adding "nobody is perfect."[1] I happen to be a professional historian, but this book has not been a history. By proceeding thematically instead of chronologically, I have tried to introduce what I see as basic issues framing the complex and sprawling topic of magic. I have also tried to draw connections between magical practices around the world. This would be impossible in any history of magic because historians revel in the specificities of time and place. Also, we simply know so much more about the history of magic in the Western world than in Asia, Africa, or the pre-colonial Americas because historians have been studying "Western civilizations" for a long time. The study of magic in the rest of the world has mainly been the purview of anthropologists, and the methods of anthropology often focus more on the present than the past. Thus, any attempt at a global history of magic would be hopelessly lopsided. There has, no doubt, still been more of a historical bent to this book than will suit some readers' tastes, and too much focus on the West. To that, I can only respond that nobody is perfect.

In this final chapter, though, I want to take a deliberately historical approach, looking only at the modern period, mainly the nineteenth through the early twenty-first century, and tracing a series of chronological developments, mainly in Western Europe and North America. This is because I see the place that magic has come to occupy in the modern world as a fundamental issue in itself. As I have frequently stressed, throughout history almost all societies have expressed at least some skepticism about certain kinds of magical practices, with different levels of skepticism often evident at different levels of society or among different social groups. Moreover, magic still exists even in the most scientifically and technologically advanced Western societies. Nevertheless, Western modernity is characterized to an unprecedented degree by the rejection of any serious belief in magic. This situation emerged from Western Europe's history and then spread around the globe because of Europe's (and the United States') political and economic domination.

I have, of course, mentioned these conditions before. They factor into many issues that I have treated in previous chapters, especially my discussion of skeptical challenges to various kinds of magic in Chapter 3. So there will be some redundancy here, as there has been throughout a book built around interlocking themes rather than straightforward progressions. Yet, a more directly historical approach will now serve to bring us to the point where magic currently stands, and so to close out the book. First, we'll look at how the modern West became so thoroughly disenchanted. Then we'll explore the various forms of magic that have subsequently developed as part of Western modernity. Finally, we'll examine how the rest of the world has confronted and in various ways accommodated the modernity that the West has exported.

## THE DISENCHANTMENT OF THE (WESTERN) WORLD

In 1917, during a talk delivered at the University of Munich, the German sociologist Max Weber proclaimed that "the fate of our times is characterized by rationalization and intellectualization and, above all, by the disenchantment of the world."[2] The word he used, *Entzauberung*, literally means de-magic-ing or, more sensibly, the removal of magic. By this, Weber meant not just the elimination of magical practices but also the increasing subjugation of all forms of transcendent spirituality and wonder to the forces of science, mechanization, and the rigid bureaucratization of modern life. Although he thought this development was a necessary part of Europe's steady progress into the future, he certainly did not consider it to be an entirely positive step, nor did many other intellectuals, and we can see a nightmare vision of an imagined techno-industrial future in Fritz Lang's classic film *Metropolis*, produced in Germany only a decade later.

In fact, magic was never eliminated from the prevailing culture of modernity, but it is certainly true that a profound marginalization of all kinds of magical practices is among the defining characteristics of modern Western society. This attitude was encapsulated in the declaration frequently made by educated Westerners in Weber's time that any serious belief in magic was inherently premodern and primitive. And since Europe was able to impose its vision of modernity on the rest of the world during its imperial heyday in the nineteenth and early twentieth centuries, disenchantment became a global force. So how did Europe get to this point?

Weber himself implied that the long, slow process of disenchantment, which had begun in antiquity, escalated with the Protestant Reformation when he incorporated the terminology of *Entzauberung* into his classic work *The Protestant Ethic and the Spirit of Capitalism*. In fact, Protestant reformers had believed very strongly in magic, especially in the malevolent power of demons and witches. One need look no further than the number of witch trials conducted by Protestant authorities in the sixteenth and seventeenth centuries. The reformers did, however, decry many Catholic rites as being superstitious, essentially magical, and therefore false. Appeal to the intercession of saints and especially the veneration of saintly relics, requiem masses said for the dead in purgatory, and a whole host of so-called sacramental items including holy water, blessed candles, and consecrated salt were stripped of their power.

While Protestant leaders still stressed the power of prayer for individual believers seeking to attain divine grace, in general Protestant theology posited a more transcendent, in some sense more distant deity than Catholicism, one less ready to intercede directly in the operation of the world on behalf of the faithful or to act through saints or earthly ministers. Protestant clergy were no longer consecrated priests wielding sacral powers. They were merely well-educated ministers whose job was to instruct others on matters of faith, not to perform elaborate rituals that invoked and manipulated spiritual forces, as Protestants believed many Catholic ceremonies and sacraments tried to do.

Exemplary of this shift is the Protestant position regarding the central Christian sacrament of the Eucharist. By the later Middle Ages, the Catholic Church had moved strongly toward the position of transubstantiation, which was declared official doctrine at the Council of Trent in 1551. During the ritual of the Mass, the substance of the Eucharist wafer was believed to transform fully into the body and blood of Christ, while maintaining the material appearance of a bit of bread. Among Protestants, Luther began to move away from this position, and subsequent reformers took the stance that the performance of the sacrament was purely symbolic and effected no real change in the substance of the Host. Thus, the Reformation marked an important shift in European thought about the meaning and power of rituals in general, including by extension magical ones.[3]

Early modern Europe's Scientific Revolution might appear to play an even greater role in disenchantment, with its focus on the natural world and stress laid on empirical observation and experimentation to arrive at the truth. As I've stressed many times, however, magic and science have frequently overlapped throughout history, and the period of the Scientific Revolution is very much a case in point. One could even go so far as to say that some major developments of early modern science were inspired by magical philosophies. When Nicholas Copernicus published his heliocentric theory in *On the Revolution of the Heavenly Spheres* just before his death in 1543, it was in many ways simpler and more elegant than the earth-centric Ptolemaic system that it aimed to challenge. Grounded in the work of the Greek astronomer Ptolemy, who lived in the second century CE, that system was weighted down with over a thousand years' worth of additions and emendations. It remained, however, a viable framework for understanding and predicting the movements of the heavens. Copernicus's system, in fact, was not based on any new empirical observations that threw Ptolemy's into confusion, and it did not immediately prove much better at accounting for observable astronomical movements. More than a generation would pass before Johannes Kepler introduced the idea of elliptical rather than perfectly circular orbits for planets, for example, that caused many pieces of the Copernican puzzle to fall into place.

So, what motivated Copernicus to make this breakthrough assertion (since it wasn't really a discovery)? As I mentioned in Chapter 3, in part, it was his attraction to the mystical and magical system of Hermetic thought flourishing at that time. Here is Copernicus from *On the Revolution of the Heavenly Spheres*, describing his vision of the cosmos: "In the middle of all sits the Sun enthroned…He is rightly called the Lamp, the Mind, the Ruler of the Universe; Hermes Trismegistus names him the visible God."[4] Hermes Trismegistus, as we've seen, was supposed to be an ancient sage who authored the mystical and magical texts of the Hermetic corpus.

Many leading figures in early modern science continued to work in areas that would now be considered magical or occult, especially astrology and alchemy. Nor did the new spirit of empirical observation always lead to skepticism about magic. In a famous debate at the end of the seventeenth century between two English scientists, John Webster, who argued against the reality of witchcraft and the power of demonic spirits, was an advocate for natural magic and occult philosophy, while Joseph Glanvill (mentioned briefly in Chapter 1) based his arguments defending the existence of witchcraft on what he considered to be solid empirical evidence for the reality of spirits.[5]

Of course, many aspects of the natural world were subject to new forms of empirical scrutiny during the Scientific Revolution, and in many areas, occult or magical explanations for natural phenomena were pushed aside. For example, natural wonders or marvelous events (everything from comets to two-headed calves) gradually ceased to be regarded as special portents sent by God to convey some hidden message and began instead to be taken as evidence of the inherent wonder of nature's not yet fully discernable design.

Even more significantly, as I already discussed in Chapter 3, a new form of natural philosophy developed during the period of the Scientific Revolution, mainly during the seventeenth century. Known as mechanical philosophy, it banished spiritual forces and occult powers entirely from the physical universe and argued that all action depended instead on direct, physical causation. I mentioned as well, however, that no less a scientific milestone than Isaac Newton's theory of gravity was derided by certain contemporaries who thought that the idea of an invisible, immaterial force permeating the universe sounded like mysticism and magic. Of course, aside from his work in physics and mathematics, Newton was also a keen student of alchemy. Some have considered this towering figure of early modern science to be "not the first of the age of reason" but "the last of the magicians."[6]

Disenchantment really took hold during the eighteenth century, as part of the intellectual movement known as the Enlightenment. Large-scale witch trials were mostly over by this time in Western Europe, and in North America as well after the powerful backlash against the Salem trials in 1692. Leading intellectuals came to believe that witchcraft could not be real because demonic spirits could not exert any real power in a mechanistic universe. By the time the special court of oyer and terminer was carrying out its executions in Massachusetts, in fact, the Dutch clergyman Balthasar Bekker had already published his *De Betoverde Weereld* (1691, translated into English as *The World Bewitched* in 1695), which made a powerful argument against any serious belief in witchcraft. Hard on Bekker's heels, the German legal theorist Christian Thomasius argued strenuously against the existence of witchcraft in his influential 1701 treatise *De crimine magiae* (On the Crime of Magic).

Over the course of the 1700s, rejection of the reality of witchcraft came to prevail among European intellectual elites. Many went on to deny not just demonic magic but divine miracles as well, arguing that an omnipotent and omniscient creator would not need to interfere constantly with his creation. This was the watchmaker-God of Enlightenment deism, winding up the mechanism of the universe at the dawn of time but then letting it run of its own accord. While some truly radical Enlightenment thinkers, especially those associated with the French Revolution, were profoundly opposed to the power of organized churches, many others were clergymen themselves. They did not want to destroy Christian faith completely, but they sought to create a religion that would harmonize with scientific reason, and they regarded belief in magic as an irrational and outmoded superstition.

Since misguided magical beliefs impeded human progress toward a fully rational society, enlightened elites worked against them every way they could: through sermons, through schooling and educational reforms, through popular pamphlet literature and eventually newspaper accounts, and especially through legal reforms that struck down old witchcraft statutes and often set up laws in their place that made it a crime to claim to be a magician, a healer, a fortune-teller, or a diviner of any sort. Of course, widespread belief in harmful witches and in other more helpful kinds of magic did not disappear overnight. In fact, they endure in Europe and North America to the present day. But it is remarkable how quickly and to what extent Western elites turned their backs on any serious magical beliefs or practices, and how they laid down rejection of magic as a cornerstone of the modern Western world.

## MODERN MAGICS

If the rejection of magic is a foundation for modernity, it is an un-stable one at best. Despite the efforts of enlightened elites, many magical beliefs and practices survived through the eighteenth century and into the nineteenth and twentieth. In Tennessee in 1947, an African-American conjure-doctor named Obie Lee Roddie treated 174 patients and earned over $2,000 through his magical craft. These details were found in his own records when police searched his dwelling after he had been murdered by a young woman who claimed that he had put a "death hex" on her. And in 1960 in Detroit, the elderly Minnie Gilland suspected her neighbor Mary Donaldson of bewitching her husband, so she used a counter-spell, a "hex sign" placed on Donaldson's house in the form of a ring of tar strewn with chicken feathers. Donaldson sued her for $75 to cover the cost of removing it.[7] On the other side of the Atlantic in 1976, Fred Mayer, a retired banker living in Hyde, Hampshire, in the south of England, received a parcel in the mail containing a chicken's heart impaled with needles. He claimed that it was a component in a spell meant to precipitate his death, and that the spell-caster was his neighbor John Baker, retired from the hardware business, with whom he had had a "year-long vendetta." Brought to Salisbury County Court, Baker denied knowing any black magic, but it was determined that he had sent the package. The judge awarded Mayer nominal damages of fifty pence, al-though he declared that "the case was the silliest he had heard in over fifteen years."[8]

Other such examples, both entertaining and sobering, could be spun out endlessly. The continuation of traditional forms of magical healing, harming, and divination in the modern Western world, however, will not be my focus here. Instead, I want to examine new magical systems that developed in the nineteenth and twentieth centuries, and show how they were integral parts of the modern culture that emerged in those years.

The Enlightenment enthronement of scientific reason as the most revered human attribute soon produced a backlash. In the arts, there was the Romantic movement, and in the realm of spirituality, there was a series of powerful religious revivals. In terms of popular interest in the occult, a major new force arose in the mid-nineteenth century from the "burned-over district" of western New York State, so called because of the many revivals that had ignited there. In 1848, the teenage Fox sisters, Kate and Margaret, living in the small township of Arcadia just east of Rochester, reported that they could communicate with spirits of the dead through audible knocking sounds that they called "rappings." They became a sensation and enjoyed great success as spirit mediums for many years. Decades later, they declared that the whole thing had been a hoax and demonstrated how they could produce rapping noises at will. By that point, however, the spiritualist movement that they had helped to start had spread across America and Europe.

In France, for example, the forces of spiritualism were harnessed by a middle-aged educator and writer who went by the pen name Allan Kardec. He created a more coherent and in his mind scientific movement known as Spiritism. Developing such methods for contacting the dead as séances, automatic writing, and spirit-photography, Kardec also drew on the legacy of Mesmerism in France to give a scientific sheen to his systems of practice. The German physician Franz Mesmer had come to Paris in the late eighteenth century and developed his theory of animal magnetism, a force that he believed was generated by all living creatures and that could be harnessed for healing and therapeutic purposes. A commission of French physicians and scientists, along with the American Ben Franklin, who was then serving as ambassador to France from the newly independent United States, declared Mesmer's theories to be unfounded, and he soon fled Paris and drifted into obscurity. Nevertheless, his ideas remained popular with those who wanted to engage with the supernatural or the spirit-world in a putatively scientific fashion.

Many people drawn to spiritualism in the nineteenth century believed that its practices offered empirical evidence of an afterlife.

The most rigorous forms of experimentation came to be known as psychical research, and in England, a Society for Psychical Research was founded in Cambridge in 1882. It soon became famous for debunking various spiritualist and occultist claims, especially when it investigated the famous Madame Blavatsky.

Helena Petrovna Blavatsky, a émigré from the Russian Empire (she was born in Ukraine and claimed Russian-German heritage), arrived in New York City in the early 1870s. In Europe, she had been deeply involved in spiritualism, but now she began to move in new directions, appropriating the term theosophy (literally, divine wisdom) for her esoteric philosophy, and founding what soon became a major organization for spiritual and occult pursuits, the Theosophical Society, with the American journalist and lawyer Henry Steel Olcott in 1875. Although grounded in spiritualism, theosophy was more overtly mystical and incorporated exotic, "oriental" elements. Specifically, Blavatsky claimed to be in contact with certain Masters of Ancient Wisdom, spiritual beings who supposedly manifested to her during her earlier travels in India. Her first major work, *Isis Unveiled* (1877), fused Western occultism with Buddhist and Hindu teachings. She and Olcott would soon move the international headquarters of the Theosophical Society to India in 1880, but the movement's base of popularity remained firmly in Europe and North America.

Blavatsky is said to have derided the Society for Psychical Research as the "Spookical Research Society."[9] They were no fans of her, either, launching an investigation into the occult phenomena she claimed to perceive or to produce, including mysterious letters "precipitated" from her hidden mahatmas. In 1885, they issued a withering dismissal of all her claims as hallucinations at best and outright frauds at worst. It would be wrong to think, however, that the Society was categorically opposed to spiritualism or other forms of occultism. Its fundamental purpose was to investigate what would now be called paranormal phenomena rigorously, and many of its members earnestly yearned to find solid, scientific proof of the existence of spirits, the afterlife, psychic powers, and occult forces.

The development of psychical research was, in fact, closely linked to psychology, just emerging as an academic discipline in the late nineteenth century and intent on fostering more scientific study of the human mind. Aside from the medical treatment of clear mental illness, the study of human thought had previously been left to philosophers. Professional psychiatrists, coming out of the medical tradition, often looked with equal disdain on both psychology and psychical research. Yet, psychiatry, too, could be said to be moving in some occult directions in the late nineteenth and early twentieth centuries, especially the psychoanalytic school, which argued that the root causes of many mental disorders lay in the newly postulated subconscious.

Sigmund Freud was a corresponding member of the Society for Psychical Research, and in his important work *The Interpretation of Dreams* (1899) he referenced both psychologists and philosophers who engaged with mysticism and the occult. Likewise, his theories about dreams and the subconscious gained considerable traction in these circles, while initially receiving less notice from the medical and psychiatric community. Freud also dabbled in the occult himself, although he did not publicize this aspect of his work for fear that it would damage his medical reputation. It is known, however, that he visited a clairvoyant in Berlin in 1909, and he organized a séance in his own house in 1913. After his death, a paper he had written taking a favorable stance toward telepathy was published in 1941.[10]

Carl Jung, Freud's great protégé, and then rival, was much more open about his engagement with the occult. At the University of Basel, he wrote his doctoral thesis on the practice of séances, published in 1902 as *On the Psychology and Pathology of So-Called Occult Phenomena*. Ultimately, he would declare that his early encounters with occultism "made it possible for me to achieve a psychological point of view." When speaking in 1919 to the Society for Psychical Research, he asserted that spiritualism and all spirit phenomena were "an appendix of psychology." And later in his life, he delved deeply into alchemy in relation to psychology.[11]

Spiritualists and psychical researchers did not think of themselves as magicians. Yet, in many other contexts, contacting the dead or tapping into spiritual forces are often considered aspects of magic. Moreover, some other modern occultists claimed very explicitly that they performed magical rites. The most famous group was the Hermetic Order of the Golden Dawn, which established its first temple in London in 1888. As a club for upper middle-class men and women (occultist groups frequently allowed women positions of considerable influence), the Golden Dawn was Masonic in structure, and Freemasonry had grown more mystical and magical over the course of the nineteenth century, incorporating elements of alchemy, Renaissance Hermeticism, and Jewish Kabbalah into its symbolism and rites.

The Golden Dawn also drew on the imagined tradition of Rosicrucianism. Supposedly founded in the fifteenth century by a German knight named Christian Rosenkreuz, this movement was first documented in the early seventeenth century in a series of pamphlets culminating in 1616 with the "Chemical Wedding of Christian Rosenkreutz." Rosicrucianism combined alchemy with Kabbalistic mysticism, and in the nineteenth century, Rosicrucian groups added elements of spiritualism to their mix of practices as well. One such group in England was the Societas Rosicruciana in Anglia, founded in 1866, and in many ways a precursor to the Golden Dawn.

In France, too, various occult societies claimed Rosicrucian roots. One major group was the Cabalistic Order of the Rosy Cross, founded in 1888. An even older occult movement was Martinism, with origins in the eighteenth century, which I mentioned in Chapter 4. Revived in the nineteenth century, it developed a particularly French concoction of Hermeticism, Mesmerism, and magic. This new Martinist Order was established in the late 1880s by Gérard Encausse, who called himself Papus, a medical doctor and specialist in psychology, and the leading French occultist of his day. He had also been involved in the Cabalistic Order of the Rosy Cross, and the Theosophical Society before that, and he would later join the Golden Dawn as well, when it opened a Paris temple.

All these groups were beholden in many ways to the Frenchman Alphonse-Louis Constant, who went by Eliphas Lévi (the Hebrew forms of his first and middle name). Trained to be a clergyman but socially radical, he grew disillusioned with the increasingly conservative bent of French society after the failed revolution of 1848, and he turned to mysticism and magic. In the mid-1850s he published his first major magical work, *Dogme et Rituel de la Haute Magie*, translated into English as *Transcendental Magic: Its Doctrine and Ritual*. Here he synthesized a rich blend of Hermeticism, Kabbalah, Mesmerism, and his own invented rites. His form of magic was highly influential on all later European occultist groups, especially the Golden Dawn.

If Lévi was the root of modern Western ritual magic, the Golden Dawn was its flowering. At first the group, like many others, focused more on the study of what it believed to be ancient systems of esoteric wisdom, but in 1892 one of its founding members, born Samuel Liddell Mathers but styling himself a descendant of Scottish aristocrats and calling himself MacGregor Mathers, established an elite inner order that would practice magic. Like so many nineteenth-century occult traditions, the rites MacGregor Mathers developed were grounded in Hermeticism and especially Kabbalistic mysticism, but they were also fluid, subject to active experimentation and improvisation.

Important as he was, Mathers was not the most influential magician associated with the Golden Dawn. That would be the infamous Aleister Crowley, although he was only a member of the organization for a few years. Born Edward Alexander Crowley (like Mathers, he too altered his name out of a fascination with all things Celtic), he joined the Golden Dawn in 1898 and was initiated into the magical second order in 1900. He soon clashed with Mathers, however, and left the group to chart his own magical course. While honeymooning in Egypt in 1904, he claimed to have been visited by an ancient Egyptian spirit from whom he received the mystical *Book of the Law*, with its central principle: "Do what thou wilt shall be the whole of the law."[12]

Crowley is famous as much for his dark reputation and for wild experiments with sex and drugs as he is for his magic. The British tabloid press dubbed him the "wickedest man in the world."[13] But his dictum to "do what thou wilt" was not an expression of unfettered hedonism. Central to Crowley's magic was his belief that each person had a True Will, essentially a spiritual calling or cosmically ordained purpose. Magical rites were meant, in part, to break down a magician's own psychic barriers to discern and then enact this will. Magic, as he defined it, was the "science and art of causing change to occur in conformity with will."[14]

With Crowley, we are deep into the world of ritual magic. He employed such age-old techniques as magical circles and triangles inscribed with mystic characters, spoke ritual invocations to summon up powerful spirits, and even sacrificed animals to access the power of their blood in his rites.[15] Nevertheless, he also keeps us in the world of psychic exploration that was an essential feature of European modernism in the early twentieth century. His magical rituals were intended to expand and in some cases to eradicate the boundaries of the magician's conscious self, his Freudian ego, and probe into the subconscious id. Crowley once wrote that he gained true insight into magic "as soon as I had destroyed my personality, as soon as I had expelled my ego."[16]

Crowley exerted tremendous influence on most systems of ritual magic that were developed after him in the modern West, but his influence on what has since become the most widespread modern magical system is "both uncertain and deeply controversial."[17] The origins of modern Witchcraft, or Wicca, can be traced to another Englishman not quite ten years Crowley's junior. Gerald Gardner launched the modern Witchcraft movement in 1954 with the publication of *Witchcraft Today*. In this book, he asserted that historical witchcraft was an ancient pagan religion, brutally repressed by Christian authorities in the medieval and early modern eras, but which had survived covertly into the twentieth century, passed down within families. He claimed that he was introduced to the faith by one such hereditary witch, whom he met while living in the south of England. In fact, Gardner created his magical system in much the same way as other nineteenth- and twentieth-century occultists did, grafting together various elements of past traditions along with his own inventions.

Born just outside Liverpool, Gardner lived most of his life abroad, mainly in Ceylon (now Sri Lanka) and Malaysia. He became interested in Eastern religions and magic, as well as in Western spiritualism. He returned permanently to England in 1936, after an early retirement from the civil service (he was only 51). Settling on the southern coast, he joined a local Rosicrucian group, as well as the academic Folklore Society and the Society for Psychical Research. In 1947, he met Crowley, who initiated him into the Ordo Templi Orientis (Order of the Eastern Temple), another group, like the Golden Dawn, focusing on ritual magic. For a brief time, Gardner worked to revive this mostly moribund organization, but he seems quickly to have lost interest and returned to developing or discovering what would become Wicca.

Various elements of ritual magic clearly made their way into Wiccan rites, but the exact lines of influence are quite murky.[18] In fact, Wicca did have a pre-Gardnerian history, insofar as the idea that historical witchcraft in Europe represented a surviving form of pagan religion long predated him. Already in the early nineteenth century, certain historians and folklorists had suggested some connection between witchcraft and pre-Christian paganism. Then, in 1862 the French historian Jules Michelet published *La sorcière* (The Witch), in which he presented an evocative, imaginary account of how a medieval peasant woman would discover magical forces in nature and so become a witch. Other historians dismissed the work, but it was widely read.

Toward the end of the nineteenth century, the wealthy American Charles Leland, an amateur folklorist, went a step beyond Michelet's historical invention and claimed to have found such a witch. While living in Florence in the 1880s, he met a woman named Maddalena, who, he claimed, practiced a pre-Christian, indeed pre-Roman, form of magical religion that had been passed down within her family. After several years, she supposedly provided him with a text recounting the beliefs and practices of this religion, which he edited and published as *Aradia or the Gospel of the Witches* (1899).

These notions of what witchcraft had been were put into their final form in England in the early twentieth century by Margaret Murray. Trained as an Egyptologist, she became a folklorist and amateur historian. She developed her depiction of witchcraft as a pagan religion in a trilogy of books: *The Witch-Cult in Western Europe* (1921), *The God of the Witches* (1933), and *The Divine King of England* (1954). For her, the practice of witchcraft focused on nature worship and rites to ensure fertility. The central figure was the so-called Horned God, whom Christian authorities took to be the devil. Despite centuries of brutal suppression, the religion survived in a remarkably coherent and organized form. In *The Divine King*, she even proposed that most English monarchs down to the seventeenth century were secretly members of the old faith. Although dismissed by professional historians, Murray's books enjoyed a broad readership. She was delighted when Gerald Gardner published his claim to have discovered a group of witches practicing what seemed to be very much the covert religion she described, and she wrote a short but approving introduction for *Witchcraft Today*.

Gardner suggested that historical witches were "Wica," or wise-people practicing beneficial magic, and this designation brought the Anglo-Saxon word *wicca* into use as an alternate term for modern Witchcraft.[19] Along with further publicizing the idea of Witchcraft as a nature-worshiping religion, Gardner developed and codified many rites in an ever-evolving text known as the Book of Shadows. In this, he was greatly helped by an early in-itiate to his religion, Doreen Valiente. She appears to have been mainly responsible for moving Witchcraft away from more patently Crowley-esque forms of ritual magic, and she began emphasizing the role of the Goddess in the religion over the Horned God.

Since the 1950s, modern Witchcraft has developed and ex-panded in remarkable ways. Almost immediately, alternate tradi-tions began to branch off from Gardner's. Valiente, for example, broke with him in the late 1950s and began charting her own course. Different strands of the movement began to draw on other components of modern Western culture. Particularly in the United States, Witchcraft, now firmly centered on Goddess-worship, took on strong feminist and environmentalist overtones. Some modern Witches continue to practice in the Gardnerian tradition, while others follow other systems, and many follow no set system at all, innovating and blending practices as they see fit. Some practice in groups (Gardner followed Murray in declaring that the ideal coven would consist of thirteen members[20]), but many are solitary practi-tioners. An endless series of guidebooks, spellbooks, and of course the internet now make every possible variety of magical rite readily available to anyone who wants to take up the craft. Through all these permutations, though, a core of modern Witchcraft has re-mained the conviction that magic is real and that rites both ancient and newly innovated can be used to access its power.

## MAGICAL MODERNITIES

Around the world, magical beliefs and practices have also contin-ued to develop in many different contexts and in many ways. One partially unifying element, however, is that these developments have frequently been shaped to at least some degree by the domi-nant form of Western modernity that denies any serious reality to magic. In fact, the perceived superiority of the modern West, not just in terms of military and industrial technology but also in its scientific rationalism and enlightened rejection of magic, helped to support and justify Western domination of the rest of the planet. Part of the self-proclaimed civilizing mission of modern imperialism was to bring the light of scientific reason to more primitive peoples who wallowed in magical superstition.

As we've seen at various points in this book, the West's exportation of its ideas about magic (that is, the dominant ideas held by its elites) began well before the modern period. As European explorers, settlers, and conquerors reached the Americas and pressed into sub-Saharan Africa and southern Asia in the sixteenth and seventeenth centuries, they saw many native practices in these regions as forms of diabolical witchcraft. In part, this was just a continuation of the ancient tendency to see the religions and rituals of other peoples as magical. While some European authorities moved immediately to eradicate these practices from regions where they had gained political control, others argued that because Native Americans, Africans, and Asians were not Christian, they could not be held culpable for their illicit magical practices in the way European witches could.

While initially it was Europe's dominant conviction that almost all magic was inherently diabolical that got exported around the globe, by the nineteenth and twentieth centuries the West was exporting disbelief. The degree to which this idea was taken up by native peoples, or by native elites who then sought to impose it on their own societies, varied quite widely. There is no way to avoid doing great injustice to the deep complexities of global history when summing up two centuries of developments in only a few pages. With that realization firmly in mind, let me nevertheless offer three models of reaction to modern disenchantment through which I'll try to frame literally a world's worth of responses.

In many ways, the easiest response is acceptance. Although the extreme rejection of all forms of magic entailed in disenchantment may run counter to deeply held tenets of any given region's native culture, Western culture exerts tremendous force. European nations came to rule much of the world in the nineteenth and early twentieth centuries, and where they didn't rule directly, they dominated in other ways. Their industries shaped economies and their schools educated governing elites. Their medical systems sought to supplant magical healing rites, while their law courts refused to recognize harmful witchcraft as a crime. And when push came to shove, as we have seen from the Zulu uprising in South Africa to the Boxer Rebellion in East Asia, their troops could brutally put down any resistance, whatever magical protections the rebels sought to deploy.

But acceptance of disenchantment was not just a matter of capitulation to Western force. Western modernity also exerted an undeniably powerful allure. A culture that provided railroads and the telegraph in the nineteenth century, and airplanes and the internet in the twentieth, was and is a culture that many people want to make their own. And since Western modernity declared, and in many ways still does, that one must give up believing in magic to be fully modern, many people have been willing to do so. In Chapter 2, I mentioned the prominent South African leader Nthato Motlana, who gave a famous speech in 1987 in which he castigated resurgent forms of traditional healing in Africa as "superstition and meaningless...mumbo jumbo," and he derided those who advocated them as trying to "lock the Black man permanently into the twelfth century."[21] A more expansive example, though, can be found in India.

As the crown jewel in Britain's imperial crown, the Indian sub-continent was the scene of far-reaching efforts both to impose modernity and to demonstrate the benefits of scientific rationalism over more traditional modes of thinking, perceived as magical and superstitious. Modern systems of communication and transportation (by 1910, British India had the fourth-largest railway network in the world, and the densest outside of Western Europe and the United States[22]) helped to create a unified state out of vast and disparate territories. Modern medicine sought to conquer tropical diseases, and public museums served to inculcate modern ways of understanding the world even where illiteracy made much of the population impervious to formal Westernized schooling. In these efforts, India's own elites were very active agents, negotiating the emergence of a modernity that could be native to the subcontinent. Part of this effort, as I noted in Chapter 1, involved purging Hinduism of what were now declared to be superstitious and magical elements to prove that scientific rationalism was as much a part of South Asia's intellectual heritage as it was of Europe's.

The situation in China is perhaps even more striking, although much less accessible to Western academics. Never reduced to the status of a European colony (except for enclaves like Hong Kong), China nevertheless felt the force of European dominance, and Chinese leaders struggled to reform and modernize their expansive empire throughout the nineteenth and early twentieth centuries. Ironically, one could argue that China was most thoroughly colonized by Western thought when its native Communist government came into power after World War II. Politically committed to scientific reason and powerfully anti-religious, Communist authorities cracked down on all aspects of what they regarded as "feudal superstitions," including many forms of traditional healing, divination, and spirit-invocation.[23] The Chinese government still regards adherence to such beliefs and practices as a form of political resistance.[24]

No matter how hard elites may struggle to eradicate what they perceive as hopelessly benighted magical superstitions, however, some segments of the population always resist, rejecting any efforts to disenchant them. Just as in Europe, so around the world systems of magic survive and in many places flourish, and they have changed and developed with the advent of a modern and now a globalized world. With the collapse of colonial governments across Africa and South Asia in the second half of the twentieth century, some regions have witnessed an aggressive rejection of disenchantment even on the part of ruling elites. I have mentioned at several points already how legal witch trials have been reinstated in some jurisdictions, while in others, authorities turn an increasingly blind eye to the lynching of suspected witches. Magical experts who traditionally provided protection from harmful witchcraft, and who for a time were subject to prosecution for defamation because of their claims to be able to identify witches, are now important witnesses in criminal cases. They frequently also serve in the entourages of the rich and powerful, and they can become quite rich and politically powerful themselves.

In rejecting disenchantment, it is important to note, these people are not rejecting modernity. Just like ritual magicians and neopagan Witches in Western societies, they live fully in the modern world. For them, however, it is a world that remains suffused with active magic that can manifest in surprising ways. One scholar of witchcraft and magic in modern Africa relates a story about how, when he was just beginning his research in the early 1970s, he attended a soccer match in the southeastern province of Cameroon. Scarcely half an hour into the match, the wife of a senior district official ran onto the field and accosted the opposing team's goalie. She was convinced that he was carrying a magical charm that was preventing her team from scoring. Sporting events are often a focus for magical activity in Cameroon, and if one wanted to see this as a remnant of archaic practices, one could draw a comparison to the use of magic in ancient forms of inter-village competition and warfare. This woman's action, however, was motivated by a very modern dynamic. Her husband was working to get the local team promoted to the First Division, which would have been a great political victory for him and a public relations coup. She was not going to allow his ambitions to be stymied by the opposing team's magic.[25]

Rather than the forces of modernization leading to anything like a "natural" decline in magical beliefs and practices, new forms of magic have emerged completely in tune with modern urbanization, industrialization, and technology. We've seen how witches are now believed to fly at night in invisible aircraft, and how a category of criminals who operate at the fringes of the modern economy, engaging in black-market swindles and internet scams, are thought to be in league with occult forces because of the mysterious origins of their money. The unprecedented and often quickly amassed new wealth available to a well-connected few due to modern economic developments, licit or otherwise, is taken by many as evidence that magic must be in operation. For example, plantation economies in both Africa and the Caribbean are sometimes rumored to operate with the help of bewitched zombie labor. Meanwhile, poor migrant workers seeking employment in other countries may turn to magic to ensure success, to protect themselves against perils abroad, or to remain connected to their families back home.[26]

The rejection of disenchantment can also become an active political statement, a declaration that post-colonial societies will not slavishly follow the blueprint for modernity developed and imposed on them by Western powers. This can lead to fraught debate between people who fully believe in magic, regarding it as an important force in their societies, and those who are honestly convinced of the superiority of scientific rationality and of the need to expunge what they see as empty superstitions. There are others, of course, who more cynically place themselves in one camp or the other for political or social advantage.

There is also a third position, beyond just acceptance or rejection of disenchantment, that can help to throw these tensions into sharper relief. In the dominant paradigm of Western modernity, disenchantment has come to mean not so much the "removal of magic" from the world as the elimination of the belief that magic could ever be real. Simply put, it posits that magic has never existed, and that people in the past were just as wrong to believe in its efficacy as modern people are. Except many people do not think this way. Scholars are becoming increasingly attentive to another position held around the world, which is that magic may indeed have been mostly expunged from Western societies, but that it remains a very real and potent force elsewhere. People in these regions may fervently want disenchantment to take place, if they feel that magic is inherently threatening or is somehow holding their society back, but they are disappointed, when they survey their situation, to see that the forces of modernity are not, in fact, eliminating magic from their world.

The anthropologist Nils Bubandt has uncovered a powerful example of this dynamic in the community of Buli, in eastern Indonesia. I've drawn specific examples from his work before, but now let me summarize this portion of his analysis. Among the Buli people, what they call *ungan* and Bubandt translates as witchcraft is an extremely serious and unpredictable threat. As in many other parts of the world, in Buli one becomes a witch when one is inhabited by a powerful entity, here called *gua*. It resides within a person, but that person will have no idea, or at least no certain idea, that it is there. The *gua* will lash out at everyone and everything around it, although never in such a way that it will positively reveal itself.

As Western modernity encroached on Buli, people were, overall, enthusiastic about the promise of disenchantment. Indeed, they very much hoped that modernization would remove the threat of witchcraft from their midst. The first clear episode in what becomes something of a saga, in Bubandt's analysis, occurred around the year 1900, when Christian missionaries arrived. They preached, or at least the natives understood them to be promising, that the new faith would mean the end of witchcraft. This was one of the main reasons that most of the population of Buli readily converted.

But witchcraft persisted, and by the 1930s, initial hopes had turned into deep resentment. Still, the inhabitants of Buli did not abandon their faith in modernity. They decided, instead, that they had misunderstood the initial message of the Westerners, and it would be other aspects of modernity, such as scientific knowledge and technology, that would eradicate the witches. As the twentieth century progressed, however, this did not play out as expected either. The last development Bubandt examines is the effort at social and political modernization undertaken as part of Indonesian President Suharto's "New Order" from the 1960s through the 1990s. This movement, too, seemed to hold out the promise of eradicating witchcraft, but it also proved a disappointment.[27]

Such aspirations and disappointments are not unique to one corner of Southeast Asia. In central Africa, the anthropologist Peter Geschiere's local assistant once confidently declared to him "where there is electric light, witchcraft will disappear." That was in 1971, but Geschiere, writing in 2013, notes that nobody would dare make such a statement anymore.[28] Even African governments have taken this position. The official *Report on the Commission of Inquiry into Witchcraft Violence and Ritual Murders* issued in 1996 by the government of the Northern Province of South Africa asserted that witchcraft had not disappeared from Europe because the inevitable advance of modernity had finally revealed its inherent unreality. Rather, early modern Europeans had taken active steps against witches. To its credit, the report suggested that South Africa should proceed by trying to reconcile witches with their communities, rather than invoking a strategy of witch-hunting and executions as Europe had used.[29]

While such debates about disenchantment take place around the globe, in the West, modern Witches are trying to re-enchant their world. Their witchcraft is a far cry from that of the Indonesian *gua*. Moreover witchcraft, however it is defined, is only one aspect of magic. And of course, not all forms of modern magic respond directly to or are shaped by the forces of modernity. Indeed, there is increasing agreement among scholars that there is no single modernity that will ultimately take uniform hold in all regions of the world. Nevertheless, the form of modernity that developed in Western Europe in the nineteenth and twentieth centuries rested heavily on the sweeping rejection of magic that emerged from the eighteenth-century Enlightenment. That disenchantment was then exported and often forcibly imposed around the globe. It has subsequently become something like a basic condition shaping many modern magical beliefs and practices, and certainly informing, although not necessarily governing, many people's perception of magic itself.

## THE END OF MAGIC?

Few scholars anymore approach history as a teleological process moving inexorably toward some predetermined end. Many people, however, and not just those in the disenchanted West, still regard belief in magic as something that human societies will eventually overcome. In fact, as we have seen in this chapter, scientific progress has no more fully eliminated magic from the modern world than did centuries of stark religious opposition in the past. Nor will magic be uniformly pushed aside as various forms of modernity advance around the globe.

I do not mean to conclude blithely that nothing much has changed. Magical beliefs and practices have undergone enormous transformations over time, and differences between cultures around the world are striking. I have, however, tried to blunt the edges of some of the crudest distinctions that might be drawn. People did not simply believe in magic in the past whereas now they don't. Nor is magic today exclusively the purview of people living in so-called developing countries in Africa, Asia, or Latin America, while sophisticated Westerners entirely reject it. At all times and in all places, people have believed in magic to varying degrees and engaged with it in various ways. Skepticism has waxed and waned and has assumed different forms in different contexts; so has the intellectual and emotional allure that magic can exert, the degree of respectability it can command, and the level of concern it can generate.

This book has tried to give some shape to the vast array of beliefs and practices that can be categorized as magic, even as it has asserted the impossibility of establishing any fixed definition for that mercurial term. It has also sought to highlight certain similarities across time and space even while noting the importance of diversity and change. In terms of the study of magic, this is not an end, but I hope readers will find that it has provided them with a good start.

# NOTES

1 Allan Megill, "The Reception of Foucault by Historians," *Journal of the History of Ideas* 48 (1987): 117–141, at 117.
2 Max Weber, "Science as a Vocation," in *From Max Weber: Essays in Sociology*, ed. and trans. Hans Heinrich Gerth and Charles Wright Mills (Oxford: Oxford University Press, 1946), 155.
3 Edward Muir, *Ritual in Early Modern Europe*, 2nd ed. (Cambridge: Cambridge University Press, 2005), 173–90.
4 Quoted in Thomas S. Kuhn, *The Copernican Revolution: Planetary Astronomy in the Development of Western Thought* (Cambridge, MA: Harvard University Press, 1957), 131.
5 Thomas Harmon Jobe, "The Devil in Restoration Science: The Glanvill-Webster Witchcraft Debate," *Isis* 72 (1981): 342–56.
6 John Maynard Keynes, "Newton, the Man," in *Newton: Tercentenary Celebrations* (Cambridge: Cambridge University Press, 1947), 27.
7 Owen Davies, *America Bewitched: The Story of Witchcraft after Salem* (Oxford: Oxford University Press, 2013), 204, 206.
8 *Times* (London), June 19, 1976, p. 3.
9 Gary Lachman, *Madame Blavatsky: The Mother of Modern Spirituality* (New York: Tarcher/Penguin, 2012), 224.
10 Corinna Treitel, *A Science for the Soul: Occultism and the Genesis of the German Modern* (Baltimore, MD: Johns Hopkins University Press, 2004), 49.
11 For his dissertation see Carl Gustav Jung, *Psychology and the Occult* (1977; reprint London: Routledge, 1982), 4–106. The quote is from Carl Gustav Jung, *Memories, Dreams, Reflections*, ed. Aniela Jaffé, trans. Richard and Clara Winston (New York: Pantheon, 1961), 107; cited in Treitel, *Science for the Soul*, 29. On his speech to the Society for Psychical Research, see Treitel, *Science for the Soul*, 49. For his work on alchemy, see e.g. Carl Gustav Jung, *Psychology and Alchemy, Vol. 12: Collected Works of C. G. Jung*, ed. and trans. Gerhard Adler and Richard Francis Carrington Hull, 2nd ed. (Princeton, NJ: Princeton University Press, 1968).
12 Richard Kaczynski, *Perdurabo: The Life of Aleister Crowley*, rev. ed. (Berkeley, CA: North Atlantic Books, 2010), 127.
13 *John Bull*, March 24, 1923; see Kaczynski, *Perdurabo*, 394.
14 Master Therion (Crowley), *Magick in Theory and Practice* (Leeds: Celephaïs Press, 2004), xii.
15 Alex Owen, *The Place of Enchantment: British Occultism and the Culture of the Modern* (Chicago, IL: University of Chicago Press, 2004), 200–201.
16 Aleister Crowley, *The Confessions of Aleister Crowley: An Autohagiography*, ed. John Symonds and Kenneth Grant (1969; reprint London: Penguin, 1989), 624; quoted in Owen, *Place of Enchantment*, 211.
17 Henrik Bogdan and Martin P. Starr, "Introduction," in *Aleister Crowley and Western Esotericism*, ed. Henrik Bogdan and Martin P. Starr (Oxford: Oxford University Press, 2012), 11.
18 The best account is Ronald Hutton, "Crowley and Wicca," in *Aleister Crowley and Western Esotericism*, ed. Henrik Bogdan and Martin P. Starr (New York: Oxford University Press, 2012), 285–306.

19 Gerald B. Gardner, *Witchcraft Today*, fiftieth anniversary edition (New York: Citadel, 2004), 102.

20 Margaret Murray, *The Witch-Cult in Western Europe* (1921; reprint New York: Barnes and Noble, 1996), 191; Gardner, *Witchcraft Today*, 114–15.

21 Quoted in Adam Ashforth, *Witchcraft, Violence, and Democracy in South Africa* (Chicago, IL: University of Chicago Press, 2005), 149.

22 Gyan Prakash, *Another Reason: Science and the Imagination of Modern India* (Princeton, NJ: Princeton University Press, 1999), 165.

23 Steve A. Smith, "Introduction," in *The Religion of Fools? Superstition Past and Present*, ed. Steve A. Smith and Alan Knight, Past & Present Supplement 3 (Oxford: Oxford University Press, 2008), 7.

24 Steve A. Smith, "Talking Toads and Chinless Ghosts: The Politics of 'Superstitious' Rumors in the People's Republic of China, 1961–1965," *American Historical Review* 111 (2006): 405–27.

25 Peter Geschiere, *The Modernity of Witchcraft: Politics and the Occult in Post-colonial Africa*, trans. Peter Geschiere and Janet Roitman (Charlottesville: University of Virginia Press, 1997), 3–4.

26 Geschiere, *Modernity of Witchcraft*, 147–48; Peter Geschiere, *Witchcraft, Intimacy, and Trust: Africa in Comparison* (Chicago, IL: University of Chicago Press, 2013), 56–57, 63–64; Kate Ramsey, *The Spirits and the Law: Vodou and Power in Haiti* (Chicago, IL: University of Chicago Press, 2011), 72–76; Lara Putnam, "Rites of Power and Rumors of Race: The Circulation of Supernatural Knowledge in the Greater Caribbean, 1890–1940," in *Obeah and Other Powers: The Politics of Caribbean Religion and Healing*, ed. Diana Paton and Maarit Forde (Durham, NC: Duke University Press, 2012), 252–53.

27 Nils Bubandt, *The Empty Seashell: Witchcraft and Doubt on an Indonesian Island* (Ithaca, NY: Cornell University Press, 2014), see esp. Chaps. 4, 6.

28 Geschiere, *Witchcraft, Intimacy, and Trust*, 2.

29 Ashforth, *Witchcraft, Violence, and Democracy*, 118.

# GLOSSARY

**Alchemy**   the art and science dealing with the purification or transformation of physical substances, most famously lead into gold.

**Amulet**   a magical item worn about the person, most often to protect against harm, magical or otherwise.

**Angel**   a messenger spirit of the Jewish, Christian, and Muslim God, typically benevolent or protective, that some magical systems claim to invoke and direct.

**Animal magnetism**   supposed natural force generated by living beings that can be manipulated to achieve therapeutic effects; the operative force in Mesmerism.

**Animism**   theory that even seemingly inanimate objects are imbued with an animating force or spirit, which often can be directed or controlled by magical rites.

**Astral magic**   magic that claims to operate by concentrating and directing forces emanating from astral bodies or of astral spirits.

**Astral projection**   supposed separation of the soul or consciousness from the body so that it can travel independently, often on another plane of existence.

**Astrology**   study of the movements of stars and other astral bodies, with the goal of making predictions based on effects they may cause on earth.

**Augury**   divination based on observation of the flight of birds; or a more general term for divination of any kind.

**Black magic**   any kind of magic that is perceived to be sinister and harmful.

**Candomblé**  syncretic religion practiced mainly in Brazil involving invocation of spirits (*orishas*), viewed by some as magical.

**Charm**  a spoken formula or material item that is thought to have magical power.

**Chiromancy**  divination by reading lines in the human hand; palm-reading.

**Common magic**  traditional, relatively basic forms of magic widespread in a given society, as opposed to learned or ritual magic; alternately called folk magic or popular magic.

**Conjure**  African-American magical tradition, focused on healing, cursing, divination, and protective charms.

**Crystal ball**  a glass ball typically associated with divination or used to contact spirits; popularized as a prop in modern stage magic.

**Cunning-folk**  practitioners of traditional forms of magical healing or divination; typically regarded as beneficial, they often provide means of protection against harmful witchcraft.

**Curse**  a magical act, often a short verbal formula, intended to cause harm or misfortune.

**Daimon**  ancient Greek term for a powerful spirit that often functioned as an agent in magical rites; sometimes still used to designate a neutral spirit, as opposed to evil demons.

**Demon**  an evil spirit that might be invoked or otherwise act as an agent in magical rites; in Judaism and Christianity, a fallen angel.

**Devil**  the chief evil spirit in Judeo-Christian-Islamic tradition; also, a generic term for any evil spirit.

**Disenchantment**  term referring of the removal of magic or more generally the widespread disbelief in magic that characterizes modern Western societies.

**Divination**  any magical system for foretelling the future or revealing otherwise hidden information.

**Emerald Tablet**  an influential Hermetic text containing a brief lists of aphorisms thought to convey mystical secrets.

**Enochian magic**  a system of ritual magic based on conjuring angelic spirits; named after the biblical figure Enoch but based on writings of the sixteenth-century English magician John Dee.

**Esotericism**   any system of beliefs, philosophies, or practices reserved for a small, specially initiated elite, including many
magical systems.

**Evil eye**   harmful power believed to be directed through a malevolent gaze.

**Exorcism**   a rite or action intended to drive evil spirits out of a
person or place.

**Familiar**   a demon or spirit in animal form serving a witch.

**Fetish**   a crafted item believed to be imbued with supernatural
power; derived from a Portuguese term (*feitiço*) applied to
West-African items of power.

**Freemasonry**   fraternal organization originating in England;
some Masonic groups came to incorporate magical elements, and forms of Freemasonry influenced many modern
European occult groups.

**Geomancy**   divination by means of earth or stones, often by patterns formed from dirt thrown across a surface.

**Gnosticism**   ancient Greek term referring to a variety of esoteric
religious systems, some of which have overlapped with or
influenced magical systems.

**Golem**   in Jewish tradition, a magically animated body made of
clay, intended to serve the magician or some other human.

**Grimoire**   a book containing formulas and instructions for performing magic.

**Hermeticism**   a magical and philosophical system based on writings attributed to Hermes Trismegistus, a supposed ancient
Egyptian sage, very influential in the European Renaissance.

**Horoscope**   a form of astrological prediction based on the position
of the stars at a particular time, typically of someone's birth.

**Incubus**   a demon in male form who has sex with a human being.

**Inquisition**   in medieval and early modern Europe, a church court
that could act against heresy, including magic and witchcraft.

**Jinn**   in Muslim traditions, a powerful spirit of a lower order than
an angel that can be invoked or otherwise operate in magical
rites.

**Kabbalah**   an esoteric system of Jewish mysticism, which in
turn influenced many magical systems, especially during the
European Renaissance.

**Learned magic**  magic entailing very specialized knowledge, usually involving complex rites often contained in texts.

**Ligature**  a magical item bound or tied to the body for healing purposes.

**Love magic**  magic used to arouse attraction or desire between two people or to destroy such desire; sometimes also magic used to promote or impede sexual potency and reproduction.

**Magi**  Persian priests and ritual experts from whom the word "magic" derives.

**Magic circle**  a ritual shape, often inscribed with symbols and characters, either drawn on paper or some other surface as part of a magical rite or drawn around a magician for protection.

**Magick**  an alternate spelling used by some modern occultists to differentiate "real magic" from stage magic.

**Medium**  a person who can contact ghosts or otherwise act as a conduit for spirits of the dead.

**Mesmerism**  a system of medical therapy developed in late eighteenth-century Europe by Anton Mesmer that claims to manipulate the supposed natural energy of animal magnetism.

**Miracle**  a supernatural occurrence caused by divine power rather than by magic.

**Natural magic**  any kind of magic drawing on forces thought to be present in nature, albeit in some hidden or occult way; e.g. astral magic.

**Necromancy**  divination by means of summoning spirits of the dead; by extension, ritual magic that operates by summoning evil spirits.

**Neo-paganism**  a variety of modern religious movements that recreate or reimagine ancient pagan forms; many are associated with the practice of magic, notably modern Witchcraft.

**Numerology**  divination by means of numbers or systems for discerning hidden meanings in numbers and number-patterns.

**Occultism**  an overarching term that can encompass most magical and esoteric traditions, referring to their general secrecy; it often refers more particularly to modern European systems of ritual magic or esoteric philosophy.

**Omen**  a sign or portent predicting some future event.

**Oracle**  a human through whom a deity communicates, especially to convey prophecies.

**Paganism**  polytheistic religions of the ancient and medieval West, and by extension elsewhere in the world, often associated by monotheistic religions with magic.

**Paranormal**  potentially referring to any occurrence outside the bounds of general scientific understanding, it most often refers to psychic phenomena like telekinesis and telepathy.

**Pentagram**  a five-pointed star, often inverted, associated with modern occultism, Satanism, and incorrectly with modern Witchcraft.

**Philosopher's stone**  a supposed alchemical substance believed to transform base metals into gold or purify the human body and extend life.

**Philter**  potion or other mixture thought to have magical properties.

**Phylactery**  a religious text or item worn on one's person; by extension a magical item worn on the body.

**Poison**  a harmful substance that injures or kills when ingested or absorbed into the body; in many societies poisoning has been closely related to witchcraft.

**Possession**  the occupation of a person, animal, or sometimes an item by a powerful spirit.

**Potion**  a liquid mixture thought to contain magical properties.

**Prayer**  a supplication of a deity or invocation of divine power, sometimes for general ends and sometimes to achieve specific purposes, in which case it can resemble a magical spell.

**Prophecy**  prediction of future events, usually thought to derive from some form of divine revelation as opposed to magical divination.

**Ritual magic**  complicated forms of magic involving elaborate or prolonged actions, often thought of as a learned art.

**Rosicrucianism**  a movement codified in seventeenth-century European literature combining alchemy with other esoteric practices (e.g. Hermeticism), promising to bring about social and spiritual transformation; influential on many later occultist groups and magical traditions.

**Runes**  Old Norse letters believed to have magical power.

**Sacrament**  a rite within a Christian church that invokes divine power, such as to confer grace.

**Santería**  a syncretic religion originating in the Caribbean involving invocation of spirits (*oirshas*) viewed by some as magical.

**Satanism**  worship of the Christian devil; a charge frequently brought against supposed witches in Christian societies. There is also a modern Satanist movement that sees itself as entirely non-Christian.

**Scrying**  the practice of conjuring visions in reflective or translucent surfaces, such as crystals, mirrors, or basins of water, usually for divination.

**Séance**  a ritual to contact spirits of the dead through a medium, central to the spiritualist movement in modern Europe and North America.

**Shaman**  a ritual expert skilled at interacting with spirts, often by traveling to spirit-realms; the term originally applied to priests and healers among northern Asian peoples.

**Sorcery**  often used as a synonym for magic or witchcraft, sometimes with a negative connotation; particularly in studies of Africa, sorcery is sometimes presented as a learned skill, in contrast to witchcraft, which is perceived as an innate power.

**Spell**  a generic term for a magical rite, typically involving spoken words, often short but potentially of any length or complexity.

**Spiritism**  a particular variety of spiritualism developed by the Frenchman Allan Kardec in the nineteenth century.

**Spiritualism**  a movement in nineteenth-century Europe and North America that maintained the reality of ghosts and possibility of communication with spirits of the dead.

**Stage magic**  illusions and sleight-of-hand tricks intended to entertain, without any claim of tapping into occult or supernatural forces.

**Succubus**  a demon in female form who seduces and has sex with a human being.

**Sympathetic magic**  magic that is believed to operate either through symbolic similarity to its desired effect (e.g. harming a doll that resembles a man harms the man), or through the principle of contagion, that things once in contact can continue to affect each other at a distance.

**Taboo**  an item or action culturally restricted from general use, usually because it has been consecrated to a deity or spirit.

**Talisman**   an item or object inscribed with symbols or characters to imbue it with magical power.

**Tarot cards**   decks of cards developed in fifteenth-century Europe; originally used as playing cards, now used primarily for divination.

**Theosophy**   an esoteric mystical and philosophical system seeking knowledge of the divine, particularly significant in modern European occultism.

**Theurgy**   magic that aims to invoke or communicate with benevolent spirits or deities.

**Trance**   a semi-conscious state in which one is more susceptible to spiritual experience.

**Vodou**   a syncretic religion originating in Haiti and associated with dancing, spirit possession, and spirit invocation.

**Wand**   a slender stick thought to focus or direct magical forces.

**White magic**   any kind of magic that is perceived to be positive and beneficial.

**Wicca**   an alternate term for modern neo-pagan Witchcraft, or in some cases for certain forms of Witchcraft, derived from the Anglo-Saxon term for a wise man or sorcerer.

**Witch doctor**   a magical specialist able to diagnose when misfortune arises from witchcraft, identify witches, and undo or provide protection from bewitchment.

**Witch hunt**   a large-scale persecution of suspected witches, usually marked by heightened levels of fear and suspicion, and the reduction or elimination of normal legal restraints.

**Witchcraft**   traditionally understood as wicked, harmful magic, often associated with women; in modern times witches are just as frequently represented as good; modern Witchcraft (capitalized) refers to the neo-pagan religion also known as Wicca.

**Witches' sabbath**   a supposed gathering of witches, typically in Christian cultures, where witches are imagined to worship the devil.

**Wizard**   a male magician, often a practitioner of elaborate ritual magic rather than simple spells or charms; in some contexts, used to designate a male witch.

**Zombie**   a reanimated corpse, in films and television often created by some viral infection, but traditionally resurrected through magic, particularly associated with Haitian Vodou.

# FURTHER READING

Most studies of magic define their scope chronologically or geographically, which is an approach this book has for the most part avoided. Nevertheless, it seems appropriate here to follow the more common divisions in the literature, rather than try to link readings artificially to my chapter divisions.

Scholarship on magic is also extremely uneven. Studies focused on medieval and early modern Europe, and especially on early modern witchcraft, are legion, and in these areas, I have limited myself mainly to listing reliable overviews. For other regions of the globe, I have listed more specialized studies that nevertheless give a sense of the shape of the field. For certain regions, I have listed the best scholarship available in English, whatever its scope.

I have categorically limited myself to books, on the assumption that these will be easier for general readers to access than scholarly articles in academic journals. I include at the end, however, a few journals that specialize in publishing academic studies of magic. I have also restricted myself entirely to material written in English or available in translation.

## THEORIES AND STRUCTURES OF MAGIC

Although much current scholarship avoids defining magic outside of specific contexts, classic anthropological and sociological works continue to be cited for the broad frameworks they offer. These include Émile Durkheim, *The Elementary Forms of Religious Life: A Study in Religious Sociology*, trans. Joseph Ward Swain (London: Allen and Unwin, 1915); James George Frazer, *The Golden Bough:*

*A Study of Magic and Religion*, abridged ed. (New York: Macmillan, 1922); Bronislaw Malinowski, *Magic, Science, and Religion, and Other Essays*, ed. Robert Redfield (Boston, MA: Beacon Press, 1948); Marcel Mauss, *A General Theory of Magic*, trans. Robert Brain (London: Routledge, 1972); and Edward Burnett Tylor, *Primitive Culture* (New York: Holt, 1889). These are usefully refined and challenged by Randall Styers, *Making Magic: Religion, Magic, and Science in the Modern World* (Oxford: Oxford University Press, 2004); and Stanley Jeyaraja Tambiah, *Magic, Science, Religion, and the Scope of Rationality* (Cambridge: Cambridge University Press, 1990). A unique collection that offers both historical and modern efforts to frame the topic of magic is Bernd-Christian Otto and Michael Stausberg, eds., *Defining Magic: A Reader* (Sheffield: Equinox, 2013).

## PSYCHOLOGY OF MAGIC

Studies addressing how magic operates within human psychology and cognitive science include Justav Jahoda, *The Psychology of Superstition* (London: Allen Lane, 1969); Jesper Sørensen, *A Cognitive Theory of Magic* (Plymouth: Altamira, 2007); Eugene Subbotsky, *Magic and the Mind: Mechanisms, Functions, and Development of Magical Thinking and Behavior* (Oxford: Oxford University Press, 2010); Stuart A. Vyse, *Believing in Magic: The Psychology of Superstition* (Oxford: Oxford University Press, 1997).

## MAGIC IN THE WESTERN WORLD

Good overviews of magic extending from Western antiquity to modern Europe include Bengt Ankarloo and Stuart Clark, eds., *Witchcraft and Magic in Europe*, 6 vols. (Philadelphia: University of Pennsylvania Press, 1999–2002): vol. 1, *Biblical and Pagan Societies*, vol. 2, *Ancient Greece and Rome*, vol. 3, *The Middle Ages*, vol. 4, *The Period of the Witch Trials*, vol. 5, *The Eighteenth and Nineteenth Centuries*, vol. 6, *The Twentieth Century*; Michael D. Bailey, *Magic and Superstition in Europe: A Concise History from Antiquity to the Present* (Lanham, MD: Rowman and Littlefield, 2007); and David J. Collins, ed., *The Cambridge History of Magic and Witchcraft in the West: From Antiquity to the Present* (Cambridge: Cambridge University

Press, 2015). Offering the slightly different perspective of esoteric studies are Arthur Versluis, *Magic and Mysticism: An Introduction to Western Esotericism* (Lanham, MD: Rowman and Littlefield, 2007); Nicholas Goodrick-Clarke, *The Western Esoteric Traditions: A Historical Introduction* (Oxford: Oxford University Press, 2008).

## MAGIC IN WESTERN ANTIQUITY

General studies that focus on Western antiquity include Gideon Bohak, *Ancient Jewish Magic: A History* (Cambridge: Cambridge University Press, 2008); Derek Collins, *Magic in the Ancient Greek World* (Oxford: Blackwell, 2008); Matthew W. Dickie, *Magic and Magicians in the Greco-Roman World* (London: Routledge, 2001); Fritz Graf, *Magic in the Ancient World*, trans. Franklin Philip (Cambridge, MA: Harvard University Press, 1997); and Daniel Ogden, *Greek and Roman Necromancy* (Princeton, NJ: Princeton University Press, 2001). On the complex interplay of cultures in late antiquity, see also Naomi Janowitz, *Magic in the Roman World: Pagans, Jews, and Christians* (London: Routledge, 2001). On how concepts of magic and magicians developed in antiquity, see Kimberly B. Stratton, *Naming the Witch: Magic, Ideology, and Stereotype in the Ancient World* (New York: Columbia University Press, 2007). On the issue of gender, see Kimberly B. Stratton and Dayna S. Kalleres, eds., *Daughters of Hecate: Women and Magic in the Ancient World* (Oxford: Oxford University Press, 2014).

## MAGIC IN MEDIEVAL EUROPE

The best overview of the entire period is Richard Kieckhefer, *Magic in the Middle Ages* (Cambridge: Cambridge University Press, 1989). Focusing only on England but offering important insights into commonplace components of magic is Catherine Rider, *Magic and Religion in Medieval England* (London: Reaktion Books, 2012). For developments associated with the rise of Christianity in the early medieval period, see Valerie I. J. Flint, *The Rise of Magic in Early Medieval Europe* (Princeton, NJ: Princeton University Press, 1991). On developments in the late medieval period, leading toward the early modern, see Frank Klaassen, *The Transformations of Magic: Illicit Learned Magic in the Later Middle Ages and Renaissance* (University

Park: Pennsylvania State University Press, 2013). The only overview of medieval Islamic magic comes in the form of a collection of articles: Emilie Savage-Smith, ed., *Magic and Divination in Early Islam* (Aldershot: Ashgate, 2004). Likewise, see Henry Maguire, ed., *Byzantine Magic* (Washington, DC: Dumbarton Oaks, 1995).

## MAGIC IN EARLY MODERN EUROPE

On Renaissance magic, classic studies include D. P. Walker, *Spiritual and Demonic Magic from Ficino to Campanella* (1958; reprint University Park: Pennsylvania State University Press, 2000); and Frances A. Yates, *Giordano Bruno and the Hermetic Tradition* (Chicago, IL: University of Chicago Press, 1964). A recent reassessment is Brian P. Copenhaver, *Magic in Western Culture: From Antiquity to the Enlightenment* (Cambridge: Cambridge University Press, 2015). On the relation of magic to the Reformation, several important studies are included in R. W. Scribner, *Religion and Culture in Germany (1400–1800)*, ed. Lyndal Roper (Leiden: Brill, 2001); while a classic work, focused on England, remains Keith Thomas, *Religion and the Decline of Magic* (New York: Scribner's, 1971). On intellectual reaction to superstition from the late medieval period through the Enlightenment, see Euan Cameron, *Enchanted Europe: Superstition, Reason, and Religion, 1250–1750* (Oxford: Oxford University Press, 2010). Various topics are addressed in Helen Parish, ed., *Superstition and Magic in Early Modern Europe: A Reader* (London: Bloomsbury, 2015). For everyday magical practices, a valuable work that ranges well beyond the early modern period is Owen Davies, *Cunning-Folk: Popular Magic in English History* (London: Hambledon and London, 2003). Also ranging beyond the early modern period is William Francis Ryan, *The Bathhouse at Midnight: A Historical Survey of Magic and Divination in Russia* (University Park: Pennsylvania State University Press, 1999).

## EARLY MODERN WITCHCRAFT AND WITCH-HUNTS

Scholarship on witchcraft far surpasses that on any other aspect of magic in early modern Europe. Numerous overviews are available, of which the best are Julian Goodare, *The European Witch-Hunt* (London: Routledge, 2016); Brian P. Levack, *The Witch-Hunt in Early Modern Europe*, 4th ed. (London: Routledge, 2016); and Brian P. Levack, ed., *The Oxford Handbook of Witchcraft in Early Modern Europe and Colonial America* (Oxford: Oxford University Press, 2013). Important studies that address the ideas and thought-processes that lay behind witchcraft, and so become informative about magical and occult thinking as a whole in early modern Europe, include Stuart Clark, *Thinking with Demons: The Idea of Witchcraft in Early Modern Europe* (Oxford: Oxford University Press, 1997); and Lyndal Roper, *Witch Craze: Terror and Fantasy in Baroque Germany* (New Haven, CT: Yale University Press, 2004). Far less has been written about witchcraft in Eastern Europe than in the West, but particularly useful as a point of comparison is Valerie Kivelson, *Desperate Magic: The Moral Economy of Witchcraft in Seventeenth-Century Russia* (Ithaca, NY: Cornell University Press, 2013).

## MAGIC AND SCIENCE

An overview that emphasizes the relationship between magic and science in medieval and early modern Europe is Steven P. Marrone, *A History of Science, Magic, and Belief: From Medieval to Early Modern Europe* (London: Palgrave, 2015). The classic work in this area remains Lynn Thorndike, *A History of Magic and Experimental Science*, 8 vols. (New York: Columbia University Press, 1923–1958). Taking a more focused approach is William Eamon, *Science and the Secrets of Nature: Books of Secrets in Medieval and Early Modern Culture* (Princeton, NJ: Princeton University Press, 1994). On alchemy, see Bruce Moran, *Distilling Knowledge: Alchemy, Chemistry, and the Scientific Revolution* (Cambridge, MA: Harvard University Press, 2005); and more broadly Lawrence M. Principe, *The Secrets of Alchemy* (Chicago, IL: University of Chicago Press, 2013). On astrology, see S. Jim Tester, *A History of Western Astrology* (Woodbridge: Boydell, 1987).

## MAGIC IN MODERN EUROPE

Scholarship on modern Europe tends to be nationally focused. The most varied work has been done on England: see Karl Bell, *Magic and Modernity in Urban England, 1780–1914* (Cambridge: Cambridge University Press, 2012); Owen Davies, *Witchcraft, Magic, and Culture*

*1736–1951* (Manchester: Manchester University Press, 1999); Tanya M. Luhrmann, *Persuasions of the Witch's Craft: Ritual Magic in Contemporary England* (Cambridge, MA: Harvard University Press, 1989); Alex Owen, *The Place of Enchantment: British Occultism and the Culture of the Modern* (Chicago, IL: University of Chicago Press, 2004). On France, see David Allen Harvey, *Beyond Enlightenment: Occultism and Politics in Modern France* (Dekalb: Northern Illinois University Press, 2005); John Warne Monroe, *Laboratories of Faith: Mesmerism, Spiritism, and Occultism in Modern France* (Ithaca, NY: Cornell University Press, 2008). On Germany, see Corinna Treitel, *A Science for the Soul: Occultism and the Genesis of the German Modern* (Baltimore, MD: Johns Hopkins University Press, 2004). An interesting study integrating modern stage magic, film, and literature is Simon During, *Modern Enchantments: The Cultural Power of Secular Magic* (Cambridge, MA: Harvard University Press, 2002). On the rise of modern Witchcraft, Ronald Hutton, *The Triumph of the Moon: A History of Modern Pagan Witchcraft* (Oxford: Oxford University Press, 1999).

## MAGIC IN GLOBAL PERSPECTIVE

There are no entirely successful overviews of magic on a global scale, although comparative work has often been attempted, particularly on witchcraft. An early collection bringing some of this work together is Mary Douglas, ed., *Witchcraft Confessions and Accusations* (London: Routledge, 1970). Subsequently, Wolfgang Behringer, *Witches and Witch-Hunts: A Global History* (Cambridge: Polity, 2004), remains largely focused on Europe with some comparative components. Peter Geschiere, *Witchcraft, Intimacy, and Trust: Africa in Comparison* (Chicago, IL: University of Chicago Press, 2013), offers an important framework for global comparisons grounded in Africa. Many studies of magic globally focus on issues of modernity, on which see Birgit Meyer and Peter Pels, eds., *Magic and Modernity: Interfaces of Revelation and Concealment* (Stanford, CA: Stanford University Press, 2003). Other studies offering global frameworks are Andrew Sanders, *A Deed without a Name: The Witch in Society and History* (Oxford: Berg, 1995); and Pamela J. Stewart and Andrew Strathern, *Witchcraft, Sorcery, Rumors, and Gossip* (Cambridge: Cambridge University Press, 2004).

## MAGIC IN AFRICA

Outside of Western Europe, more studies of magic focus on Africa than any other global region. Most often these studies concentrate on the issue of witchcraft. There is, however, no reliable overview that covers the entire continent. A classic work is Edward Evan Evans-Pritchard, *Witchcraft, Oracles and Magic among the Azande* (Oxford: Clarendon, 1937). More recent studies include Adam Ashforth, *Witchcraft, Violence, and Democracy in South Africa* (Chicago, IL: University of Chicago Press, 2005); Clifton Crais, *Magic, State Power and the Political Imagination in South Africa* (Cambridge: Cambridge University Press, 2002); Peter Geschiere, *The Modernity of Witchcraft: Politics and the Occult in Postcolonial Africa*, trans. Peter Geschiere and Janet Roitman (Charlottesville: University of Virginia Press, 1997); Henriette L. Moore and Todd Sanders, eds., *Magical Interpretations, Material Realities: Modernity, Witchcraft and the Occult in Postcolonial Africa* (London: Routledge, 2001).

## MAGIC IN ASIA

Relatively little scholarship has focused on magic across Asia. No overviews are available, even for major regions, but some good focused studies include Nils Bubandt, *The Empty Seashell: Witchcraft and Doubt on an Indonesian Island* (Ithaca, NY: Cornell University Press, 2014); Barend J. ter Haar, *Telling Stories: Witchcraft and Scapegoating in Chinese History* (Leiden: Brill, 2006); Philip A. Kuhn, *Soulstealers: The Chinese Sorcery Scare of 1768* (Cambridge, MA: Harvard University Press, 1990); Margaret J. Wiener, *Visible and Invisible Realms: Power, Magic, and Colonial Conquest in Bali* (Chicago, IL: University of Chicago Press, 1995).

## MAGIC IN CENTRAL AND SOUTH AMERICA

Studies focusing on the colonial period include Fernando Cervantes, *The Devil in the New World: The Impact of Diabolism in New Spain* (New Haven, CT: Yale University Press, 1994); Irene Silverblatt, *Moon, Sun, and Witches: Gender Ideologies and Class in Inca and Colonial Peru* (Princeton, NJ: Princeton University Press,

1987); and Laura de Mello e Souza, *The Devil and the Land of the Holy Cross: Witchcraft, Slavery, and Popular Religion in Colonial Brazil*, trans. Diane Grosklaus Whitty (Austin: University of Texas Press, 2003). Covering both the colonial and post-colonial period is Luis Nicolau Parés and Roger Sansi, eds., *Sorcery in the Black Atlantic* (Chicago, IL: University of Chicago Press, 2011). Studies of the modern Caribbean region include Diana Paton and Maarit Forde, eds., *Obeah and Other Powers: The Politics of Caribbean Religion and Healing* (Durham, NC: Duke University Press, 2012); Kate Ramsey, *The Spirits and the Law: Vodou and Power in Haiti* (Chicago, IL: University of Chicago Press, 2011); and Raquel Romberg, *Witchcraft and Welfare: Spiritual Capital and the Business of Magic in Modern Puerto Rico* (Austin: University of Texas Press, 2003).

## MAGIC IN NORTH AMERICA

Studies of magic in North America are quite diverse. The largest number by far focus on witchcraft in colonial New England, which is, in most regards, an extension of early modern European witchcraft. A useful overview is John Demos, *The Enemy Within: 2,000 Years of Witch-Hunting in the Western World* (New York: Viking, 2008) (despite its title, it is overwhelmingly about colonial America). Important studies that move beyond witch-hunting to consider magic more generally are Richard Godbeer, *The Devil's Dominion: Magic and Religion in Early New England* (Cambridge: Cambridge University Press, 1992); and David D. Hall, *Worlds of Wonder, Days of Judgment: Popular Religious Belief in Early New England* (Cambridge, MA: Harvard University Press, 1990). An attempt to integrate Native American magic, as well as French and Spanish colonial territories, is Alison Games, *Witchcraft in Early North America* (Lanham, MD: Rowman and Littlefield, 2010). An informative study focused entirely on one Native American society is Matthew Dennis, *Seneca Possessed: Indians, Witchcraft, and Power in the Early American Republic* (Philadelphia: University of Pennsylvania Press, 2010). On African-American magical traditions, see Yvonne P. Chireau, *Black Magic: Religion and the African-American Conjuring Tradition* (Berkeley: University of California Press, 2003). The other great focus of scholarship is on modern spiritualism, occultism, and neo-pagan Witchcraft. For an over-view, see Helen A. Berger, ed., *Witchcraft and Magic: Contemporary North America* (Philadelphia: University of Pennsylvania Press, 2005). A classic account is Margot Adler, *Drawing Down the Moon: Witches, Druids, Goddess-Worshippers, and Other Pagan Religions in America Today*, rev. ed. (New York: Penguin/Arkana, 1986).

## MAGICAL TEXTS

A wide assortment of magical texts and texts addressing magic are available from many different periods. The broadest collection is now Brian Copenhaver, *The Book of Magic: From Antiquity to the Enlightenment* (London: Penguin, 2015). Specifically, for the an-cient Western world, see Hans Dieter Betz, ed., *The Greek Magical Papyri in Translation, Including the Demotic Spells*, 2nd ed. (Chicago, IL: University of Chicago Press, 1992); Georg Luck, *Arcana Mundi: Magic and the Occult in the Greek and Roman Worlds, A Collection of Ancient Texts*, 2nd ed. (Baltimore, MD: Johns Hopkins University Press, 2006); or Marvin Meyer and Richard Smith, *Ancient Christian Magic: Coptic Texts of Ritual Power* (New York: Harper Collins, 1994). On European witchcraft, see Alan Charles Kors and Edward Peters, eds., *Witchcraft in Europe 400–1700: A Documentary History*, 2nd ed. (Philadelphia: University of Pennsylvania Press, 2001); or Brian P. Levack, ed., *The Witchcraft Sourcebook*, 2nd ed. (New York: Routledge, 2015). Extending beyond witchcraft are Peter G. Maxwell-Stuart, ed., *The Occult in Early Modern Europe: A Documentary History* (New York: St. Martin's, 1999); and Peter G. Maxwell-Stuart, ed., *The Occult in Medieval Europe, 500–1500: A Documentary History* (New York: Palgrave Macmillan, 2005). Many texts are available on modern magic and occultism. Influential ex-amples dealing with ritual magic include Éliphas Lévi, *Transcen-dental Magic: Its Doctrine and Ritual*, trans. Arthur Edward Waite (London: Rider and Co., 1896); and Master Therion (Aleister Crowley), *Magick in Theory and Practice* (London: n.p., 1929). On modern Witchcraft, see Charles G. Leland, *Aradia, or the Gospel of the Witches* (London: D. Nutt, 1899); and Starhawk, *The Spiral Dance: A Rebirth of the Ancient Religion of the Great Goddess*, 20th-anniversary edition (New York: HarperCollins, 1999).

## JOURNALS

Several academic journals focus on magic or aspects of magic. They are useful both for their articles and for reviews of the most recent books in the field. They include *Aries: Journal for the Study of Western Esotericism* (E. J. Brill); *Magic, Ritual, and Witchcraft* (University of Pennsylvania Press); *The Pomegranate: The International Journal of Pagan Studies* (Equinox Press); *Preternature: Critical and Historical Studies of the Preternatural* (Pennsylvania State University Press).

# INDEX

Printed in the United States
by Baker & Taylor Publisher Services